# MznLnx

*Missing Links Exam Preps*

Exam Prep for

# Chapter Zero: Fundamental Notions of Abstract Mathematics

Schumacher, 2nd Edition

The MznLnx Exam Prep is your link from the texbook and lecture to your exams.
The MznLnx Exam Preps are unauthorized and comprehensive reviews of your textbooks.

All material provided by MznLnx and Rico Publications (c) 2010
Textbook publishers and textbook authors do not particpate in or contribute to these reviews.

## MznLnx

## Rico Publications

*Exam Prep for Chapter Zero: Fundamental Notions of Abstract Mathematics*
2nd Edition
Schumacher

*Publisher:* Raymond Houge
*Assistant Editor:* Michael Rouger
*Text and Cover Designer:* Lisa Buckner
*Marketing Manager:* Sara Swagger
*Project Manager, Editorial Production:* Jerry Emerson
*Art Director:* Vernon Lowerui

*Product Manager:* Dave Mason
*Editorial Assitant:* Rachel Guzmanji
*Pedagogy:* Debra Long
*Cover Image:* Jim Reed/Getty Images
*Text and Cover Printer:* City Printing, Inc.
*Compositor:* Media Mix, Inc.

(c) 2010 Rico Publications

ALL RIGHTS RESERVED. No part of this work covered by the copyright may be reproduced or used in any form or by an means--graphic, electronic, or mechanical, including photocopying, recording, taping, Web distribution, information storage, and retrieval systems, or in any other manner--without the written permission of the publisher.

Printed in the United States
ISBN:

For more information about our products, contact us at:
Dave.Mason@RicoPublications.com

For permission to use material from this text or product, submit a request online to:
Dave.Mason@RicoPublications.com

# Contents

**CHAPTER 1**
*Logic* — 1

**CHAPTER 2**
*Sets* — 7

**CHAPTER 3**
*Induction* — 14

**CHAPTER 4**
*Relations* — 16

**CHAPTER 5**
*Functions* — 28

**CHAPTER 6**
*Elementary Number Theory* — 37

**CHAPTER 7**
*Cardinality* — 47

**CHAPTER 8**
*The Real Numbers* — 57

**ANSWER KEY** — 74

# TO THE STUDENT

## COMPREHENSIVE

The *MznLnx* Exam Prep series is designed to help you pass your exams. Editors at MznLnx review your textbooks and then prepare these practice exams to help you master the textbook material. Unlike study guides, workbooks, and practice tests provided by the texbook publisher and textbook authors, *MznLnx* gives you **all** of the material in each chapter in exam form, not just samples, so you can be sure to nail your exam.

## MECHANICAL

The MznLnx Exam Prep series creates exams that will help you learn the subject matter as well as test you on your understanding. Each question is designed to help you master the concept. Just working through the exams, you gain an understanding of the subject--its a simple mechanical process that produces success.

## INTEGRATED STUDY GUIDE AND REVIEW

MznLnx is not just a set of exams designed to test you, its also a comprehensive review of the subject content. Each exam question is also a review of the concept, making sure that you will get the answer correct without having to go to other sources of material. You learn as you go! Its the easiest way to pass an exam.

## HUMOR

Studying can be tedious and dry. MznLnx's instructional design includes moderate humor within the exam questions on occassion, to break the tedium and revitalize the brain

## Chapter 1. Logic

1. In traditional logic, an _____ or postulate is a proposition that is not proved or demonstrated but considered to be either self-evident, or subject to necessary decision. Therefore, its truth is taken for granted, and serves as a starting point for deducing and inferring other truths.

   In mathematics, the term _____ is used in two related but distinguishable senses: 'logical _____s' and 'non-logical _____s'.

   a. Enumerative definition
   b. Algebraic logic
   c. Axiom
   d. AND-OR-Invert

2. In mathematics, a _____ is a statement that can be proved on the basis of explicitly stated or previously agreed assumptions.
   a. Disjunction introduction
   b. Theorem
   c. Logical value
   d. Boolean function

3. _____ is a mathematical system attributed to the Greek mathematician Euclid of Alexandria. Euclid's Elements is the earliest known systematic discussion of geometry. It has been one of the most influential books in history, as much for its method as for its mathematical content.
   a. Infinitely near point
   b. Equidimensional
   c. Analytic geometry
   d. Euclidean geometry

4. In mathematics, _____ describes hyperbolic and elliptic geometry, which are contrasted with Euclidean geometry. The essential difference between Euclidean and _____ is the nature of parallel lines. Euclid's fifth postulate, the parallel postulate, is equivalent to Playfair's postulate, which states that, within a two-dimensional plane, for any given line l and a point A, which is not on l, there is exactly one line through A that does not intersect l.
   a. Tropical geometry
   b. Nash function
   c. Brascamp-Lieb inequality
   d. Non-Euclidean geometry

## Chapter 1. Logic

5. _____ is a part of mathematics concerned with questions of size, shape, and relative position of figures and with properties of space. _____ is one of the oldest sciences. Initially a body of practical knowledge concerning lengths, areas, and volumes, in the third century BC _____ was put into an axiomatic form by Euclid, whose treatment--Euclidean _____--set a standard for many centuries to follow.

   a. Geometry
   b. 120-cell
   c. 2-3 heap
   d. 1-center problem

6. In mathematics, a _____ is a convincing demonstration that some mathematical statement is necessarily true. _____s are obtained from deductive reasoning, rather than from inductive or empirical arguments. That is, a _____ must demonstrate that a statement is true in all cases, without a single exception.

   a. Congruent
   b. Conchoid
   c. Germ
   d. Proof

7. In mathematics, a group G is called _____ if there is a subset S of G such that any element of G can be written in one and only one way as a product of finitely many elements of S and their inverses.

   A related but different notion is a _____ abelian group.

   _____ groups first arose in the study of hyperbolic geometry, as examples of Fuchsian groups.

   a. Boolean algebra
   b. Free
   c. Leibniz formula
   d. Barycentric coordinates

8. In mathematics, and in other disciplines involving formal languages, including mathematical logic and computer science, a _____ is a notation that specifies places in an expression where substitution may take place. The idea is related to a placeholder, or a wildcard character that stands for an unspecified symbol.

   The variable x becomes a bound variable, for example, when we write

   'For all $x, ^2 = x^2 + 2x + 1$.'

or

'There exists x such that $x^2 = 2$.'

In either of these propositions, it does not matter logically whether we use x or some other letter.

   a. 2-3 heap
   b. Free variable
   c. 120-cell
   d. 1-center problem


9. _____ is the study of the principles of valid demonstration and inference. _____ is a branch of philosophy, a part of the classical trivium of grammar, _____, and rhetoric. of λογικῌς, 'possessed of reason, intellectual, dialectical, argumentative', from λῐΌγος logos, 'word, thought, idea, argument, account, reason, or principle'.
   a. Counterpart theory
   b. Logic
   c. Boolean function
   d. Satisfiability


10. In logic and mathematics, or, also known as logical _____ or inclusive _____ is a logical operator that results in true whenever one or more of its operands are true. In grammar, or is a coordinating conjunction. In ordinary language 'or' rather has the meaning of exclusive _____.
   a. Triquetra
   b. Disjunction
   c. Cube
   d. Zero-point energy


11. In logic and mathematics, _____ or not is an operation on logical values, for example, the logical value of a proposition, that sends true to false and false to true. Intuitively, the _____ of a proposition holds exactly when that proposition does not hold. In grammar, nor is an adverb which acts as a coordinating conjunction.
   a. Sentence diagram
   b. Negation
   c. Syntax
   d. 1-center problem

12. A _____ is a mathematical table used in logic -- specifically in connection with Boolean algebra, boolean functions, and propositional calculus -- to compute the functional values of logical expressions on each of their functional arguments, that is, on each combination of values taken by their logical variables. In particular, _____s can be used to tell whether a propositional expression is true for all legitimate input values, that is, logically valid.

The pattern of reasoning that the _____ tabulates was Frege's, Peirce's, and Schröder's by 1880.

   a. 120-cell
   b. 2-3 heap
   c. 1-center problem
   d. Truth table

13. In mathematics, an _____ is a theorem with a statement beginning 'there exis ..' y, ... there exis ...'. That is, in more formal terms of symbolic logic, it is a theorem with a statement involving the existential quantifier.
   a. A Mathematical Theory of Communication
   b. Existence theorem
   c. A posteriori
   d. A chemical equation

14. In mathematics and logic, the phrase 'there is one and only one' is used to indicate that exactly one object with a certain property exists. In mathematical logic, this sort of quantification is known as _____ quantification or unique existential quantification.

_____ quantification is often denoted with the symbols '∃!' or ∃$_{=1}$'.

   a. A posteriori
   b. A chemical equation
   c. A Mathematical Theory of Communication
   d. Uniqueness

15. Induction or _____, sometimes called inductive logic, is the process of reasoning in which the premises of an argument are believed to support the conclusion but do not entail it;. Induction is a form of reasoning that makes generalizations based on individual instances. It is used to ascribe properties or relations to types based on an observation instance; or to formulate laws based on limited observations of recurring phenomenal patterns.
   a. Affine logic
   b. Idempotency of entailment
   c. Intuitionistic logic
   d. Inductive reasoning

## Chapter 1. Logic

16. In mathematics and logic, a _____ is a way of showing the truth or falsehood of a given statement by a straightforward combination of established facts, usually existing lemmas and theorems, without making any further assumptions. In order to directly prove a conditional statement of the form 'If p, then q', it is only necessary to consider situations where the statement p is true. Logical deduction is employed to reason from assumptions to conclusion.

   a. Direct proof
   b. Minimal counterexample
   c. Proofs from THE BOOK
   d. Proof by exhaustion

17. In propositional logic, contraposition is a logical relationship between two statements of material implication. A proposition Q is materially implicated by a proposition P when the following relationship holds:

$$(P \rightarrow Q)$$

In vernacular terms, this states 'If P then Q', or, 'If Socrates is a man then Socrates is human.' In a conditional such as this, P is called the antecedent and Q the consequent. One statement is the _____ of the other just when its antecedent is the negated consequent of the other, and vice-versa.

   a. Contour map
   b. Contrapositive
   c. Continuous signal
   d. Control chart

18. _____ reductio ad impossibile is a type of logical argument where one assumes a claim for the sake of argument and derives an absurd or ridiculous outcome, and then concludes that the original claim must have been wrong as it led to an absurd result.

It makes use of the law of non-contradiction -- a statement cannot be both true and false. In some cases it may also make use of the law of excluded middle -- a statement must be either true or false.

   a. 1-center problem
   b. 120-cell
   c. Reductio ad absurdum
   d. 2-3 heap

19. In mathematics, a _____ is a mathematical statement which appears resourceful, but has not been formally proven to be true under the rules of mathematical logic. Once a _____ is formally proven true it is elevated to the status of theorem and may be used afterwards without risk in the construction of other formal mathematical proofs. Until that time, mathematicians may use the _____ on a provisional basis, but any resulting work is itself provisional until the underlying _____ is cleared up.
   a. Heawood conjecture
   b. Moral certainty
   c. Conjecture
   d. Whitehead conjecture

## Chapter 2. Sets

1. In abstract algebra, the _____, named after the ancient Greek mathematician Archimedes of Syracuse, is a property held by some groups, fields, and other algebraic structures. Roughly speaking, it is the property of having no infinitely large or infinitely small elements. This can be made precise in various contexts, for example, for fields with an absolute value, where the ordered field of real numbers is Archimedean, but the field of p-adic numbers with the p-adic absolute value is non-Archimedean.
    a. Algebraic closure
    b. Archimedean property
    c. Isomorphism extension theorem
    d. Embedding problem

2. In mathematics, the _____ is a direct product of sets. The _____ is named after René Descartes, whose formulation of analytic geometry gave rise to this concept.

    Specifically, the _____ of two sets X and Y, denoted X × Y, is the set of all possible ordered pairs whose first component is a member of X and whose second component is a member of Y:

    $$X \times Y = \{(x,y) | x \in X \text{ and } y \in Y\}.$$

    For example, the _____ of the 13-element set of standard playing card ranks {Ace, King, Queen, Jack, 10, 9, 8, 7, 6, 5, 4, 3, 2} and the four-element set of card suits {♠, ♥, ♦, ♣} is the 52-element set of all possible playing cards ,, ...,, ....,}.

    a. Choice function
    b. Set of all sets
    c. Disjoint sets
    d. Cartesian product

3. The _____ are the set of numbers consisting of the natural numbers including 0 and their negatives. They are numbers that can be written without a fractional or decimal component, and fall within the set {... −2, −1, 0, 1, 2, ...}.
    a. A Mathematical Theory of Communication
    b. A chemical equation
    c. A posteriori
    d. Integers

4. In mathematics, a _____ can mean either an element of the set {1, 2, 3, ...} or an element of the set {0, 1, 2, 3, ...}. The latter is especially preferred in mathematical logic, set theory, and computer science.

    _____s have two main purposes: they can be used for counting, and they can be used for ordering.

## Chapter 2. Sets

  a. Suslin cardinal
  b. Cardinal numbers
  c. Strong partition cardinal
  d. Natural number


5. In mathematics, a _____ is a number which can be expressed as a ratio of two integers. Non-integer _____s are usually written as the vulgar fraction $\frac{a}{b}$, where b is not zero. a is called the numerator, and b the denominator.
  a. Pre-algebra
  b. Tally marks
  c. Minkowski distance
  d. Rational number


6. _____ is the branch of mathematics that studies sets, which are collections of objects. Although any type of objects can be collected into a set, _____ is applied most often to objects that are relevant to mathematics.

The modern study of _____ was initiated by Cantor and Dedekind in the 1870s.

  a. Logical conjunction
  b. Consistent
  c. Logical value
  d. Set theory


7. In mathematics, a _____ is, informally, an infinitely vast and infinitely thin sheet. _____s may be thought of as objects in some higher dimensional space, or they may be considered without any outside space, as in the setting of Euclidean geometry
  a. Bandwidth
  b. Group
  c. Blocking
  d. Plane


8. In mathematics, the _____s may be described informally in several different ways. The _____s include both rational numbers, such as 42 and −23/129, and irrational numbers, such as pi and the square root of two; or, a _____ can be given by an infinite decimal representation, such as 2.4871773339...., where the digits continue in some way; or, the _____s may be thought of as points on an infinitely long number line.

These descriptions of the _____s, while intuitively accessible, are not sufficiently rigorous for the purposes of pure mathematics.

## Chapter 2. Sets

a. Minkowski distance
b. Tally marks
c. Pre-algebra
d. Real number

9. The word _____ has many distinct meanings in different fields of knowledge, depending on their methodologies and the context of discussion. Broadly speaking we can say that a _____ is some kind of belief or claim that (supposedly) explains, asserts, or consolidates some class of claims. Additionally, in contrast with a theorem the statement of the _____ is generally accepted only in some tentative fashion as opposed to regarding it as having been conclusively established.

a. Per mil
b. Transport of structure
c. Defined
d. Theory

10. In mathematics, an _____ or member of a set is any one of the distinct objects that make up that set.

Writing A = {1,2,3,4}, means that the _____s of the set A are the numbers 1, 2, 3 and 4. Groups of _____s of A, for example {1,2}, are subsets of A.

a. Order
b. Element
c. Universal code
d. Ideal

11. In mathematics, and more specifically set theory, the _____ is the unique set having no members. Some axiomatic set theories assure that the _____ exists by including an axiom of _____; in other theories, its existence can be deduced. Many possible properties of sets are trivially true for the _____.

a. Inverse function
b. Empty function
c. A Mathematical Theory of Communication
d. Empty set

12. In mathematics, a _____ is a set of real numbers with the property that any number that lies between two numbers in the set is also included in the set. For example, the set of all numbers x satisfying $0 \leq x \leq 1$ is an _____ which contains 0 and 1, as well as all numbers between them. Other examples of _____s are the set of all real numbers $\mathbb{R}$, the set of all positive real numbers, and the empty set.

a. Order
b. Annihilator
c. Ideal
d. Interval


13. _____ is the notation in which permitted values for a variable are expressed as ranging over a certain interval; "5 < x < 9" is an example of the application of _____.
    a. Infinity
    b. A Mathematical Theory of Communication
    c. Implicit differentiation
    d. Interval notation


14. In mathematics, especially in set theory, a set A is a _____ of a set B if A is 'contained' inside B. Notice that A and B may coincide. The relationship of one set being a _____ of another is called inclusion.
    a. Horizontal line test
    b. Set of all sets
    c. Cartesian product
    d. Subset


15. In discrete mathematics and predominantly in set theory, a _____ is a concept used in comparisons of sets to refer to the unique values of one set in relation to another. The terms 'absolute' and 'relative' _____ refer to more specific applications of the concept, with universal _____s referring to elements unique to the universal set and the latter referring to the unique elements of one set in relation to another. In this image, the universal set is represented by the border of the image, and the set A as a disc.
    a. Derivative algebra
    b. Huge
    c. Kernel
    d. Complement


16. In mathematics, the _____ of two sets A and B is the set that contains all elements of A that also belong to B, but no other elements.

For explanation of the symbols used in this article, refer to the table of mathematical symbols.

The _____ of A and B

The _____ of A and B is written 'A ∩ B'. Formally:

x is an element of A ∩ B if and only if
- x is an element of A and
- x is an element of B.

For example:
- The _____ of the sets {1, 2, 3} and {2, 3, 4} is {2, 3}.
- The number 9 is not in the _____ of the set of prime numbers {2, 3, 5, 7, 11, …} and the set of odd numbers {1, 3, 5, 7, 9, 11, …}.

If the _____ of two sets A and B is empty, that is they have no elements in common, then they are said to be disjoint, denoted: A ∩ B = ∅. For example the sets {1, 2} and {3, 4} are disjoint, written {1, 2} ∩ {3, 4} = ∅.

a. Order
b. Erlang
c. Advice
d. Intersection

17. In set theory, the term _____ refers to a set operation used in the convergence of set elements to form a resultant set containing the elements of both sets. As a simple example, a _____ of two disjoint sets, which do not have elements in common results in a set containing all elements from both sets. A Venn diagram representing the _____ of sets A and B.

a. Event
b. Union
c. Introduction
d. UES

18. _____ or set diagrams are diagrams that show all hypothetically possible logical relations between a finite collection of sets. _____ were invented around 1880 by John Venn. They are used in many fields, including set theory, probability, logic, statistics, and computer science.

a. 1-center problem
b. 120-cell
c. 2-3 heap
d. Venn diagrams

19. In traditional logic, an _____ or postulate is a proposition that is not proved or demonstrated but considered to be either self-evident, or subject to necessary decision. Therefore, its truth is taken for granted, and serves as a starting point for deducing and inferring other truths.

In mathematics, the term _____ is used in two related but distinguishable senses: 'logical _____s' and 'non-logical _____s'.

a. Algebraic logic
b. AND-OR-Invert
c. Enumerative definition
d. Axiom

20. A _____ is a 2D geometric symbolic representation of information according to some visualization technique. Sometimes, the technique uses a 3D visualization which is then projected onto the 2D surface. The word graph is sometimes used as a synonym for _____.

a. 120-cell
b. 1-center problem
c. 2-3 heap
d. Diagram

21. In mathematics, given a set S, the _____ of S, written $\mathcal{P}(S)$, PS, is the set of all subsets of S. In axiomatic set theory, the existence of the _____ of any set is postulated by the axiom of _____.

Any subset F of $\mathcal{P}(S)$ is called a family of sets over S.

a. Power set
b. Polarization
c. Formal derivative
d. Formal power series

22. In set theory, a _____ (or discriminated union) is a modified union operation which indexes the elements according to which set they originated in.

Formally, let {$A_i$ : i ∈ I} be a family of sets indexed by I. The _____ of this family is the set

$$\coprod_{i \in I} A_i = \bigcup_{i \in I} \{(x, i) : x \in A_i\}.$$

The elements of the _____ are ordered pairs (x, i.)

a. Preimage
b. Cartesian product
c. Disjoint sets
d. Disjoint union

## Chapter 3. Induction

1. _____ is a method of mathematical proof typically used to establish that a given statement is true of all natural numbers. It is done by proving that the first statement in the infinite sequence of statements is true, and then proving that if any one statement in the infinite sequence of statements is true, then so is the next one.

The method can be extended to prove statements about more general well-founded structures, such as trees; this generalization, known as structural induction, is used in mathematical logic and computer science.

   a. Mathematical induction
   b. Finitary
   c. Herbrand structure
   d. Ground expression


2. In traditional logic, an _____ or postulate is a proposition that is not proved or demonstrated but considered to be either self-evident, or subject to necessary decision. Therefore, its truth is taken for granted, and serves as a starting point for deducing and inferring other truths.

In mathematics, the term _____ is used in two related but distinguishable senses: 'logical _____s' and 'non-logical _____s'.

   a. Enumerative definition
   b. AND-OR-Invert
   c. Algebraic logic
   d. Axiom


3. In mathematics and computer science, _____ (also base-16, hexa or base, of 16. It uses sixteen distinct symbols, most often the symbols 0-9 to represent values zero to nine, and A, B, C, D, E, F (or a through f) to represent values ten to fifteen.

Its primary use is as a human friendly representation of binary coded values, so it is often used in digital electronics and computer engineering.

   a. Hexadecimal
   b. Tetradecimal
   c. Factoradic
   d. Radix


4. In mathematical analysis, a metric space M is said to be _____ (or Cauchy) if every Cauchy sequence of points in M has a limit that is also in M or alternatively if every Cauchy sequence in M converges in M.

Intuitively, a space is _____ if there are no 'points missing' from it (inside or at the boundary.) For instance, the set of rational numbers is not _____, because $\sqrt{2}$ is 'missing' from it, even though one can construct a Cauchy sequence of rational numbers that converges to it.

a. 120-cell
b. Complete
c. 1-center problem
d. 2-3 heap

# Chapter 4. Relations

1. In mathematics, the _____ is a direct product of sets. The _____ is named after René Descartes, whose formulation of analytic geometry gave rise to this concept.

Specifically, the _____ of two sets X and Y, denoted X × Y, is the set of all possible ordered pairs whose first component is a member of X and whose second component is a member of Y:

$$X \times Y = \{(x,y) | x \in X \text{ and } y \in Y\}.$$

For example, the _____ of the 13-element set of standard playing card ranks {Ace, King, Queen, Jack, 10, 9, 8, 7, 6, 5, 4, 3, 2} and the four-element set of card suits {♠, ♥, ♦, ♣} is the 52-element set of all possible playing cards ,, ...,,, ...,,}.

   a. Cartesian product
   b. Set of all sets
   c. Choice function
   d. Disjoint sets

2. In quantum field theory and statistical mechanics in the thermodynamic limit, a system with a global symmetry can have more than one phase. For parameters where the symmetry is spontaneously broken, the system is said to be _____. When the global symmetry is unbroken the system is disordered.
   a. Isoenthalpic-isobaric ensemble
   b. Einstein relation
   c. Ursell function
   d. Ordered

3. In mathematics, an _____ is a collection of objects having two coordinates (or entries or projections), such that one can always uniquely determine the object, which is the first coordinate (or first entry or left projection) of the pair as well as the second coordinate (or second entry or right projection.) If the first coordinate is a and the second is b, the usual notation for an _____ is (a, b.) The pair is 'ordered' in that (a, b) differs from (b, a) unless a = b.
   a. Ordered pair
   b. A Mathematical Theory of Communication
   c. A posteriori
   d. A chemical equation

4. In mathematics, a _____ is, informally, an infinitely vast and infinitely thin sheet. _____s may be thought of as objects in some higher dimensional space, or they may be considered without any outside space, as in the setting of Euclidean geometry

a. Blocking
b. Bandwidth
c. Group
d. Plane

5. In mathematics, a binary relation R on a set X is _____ if, for all a and b in X, if a is R to b and b is R to a, then a = b.

In mathematical notation, this is:

$$\forall a, b \in X,\ aRb \wedge bRa \Rightarrow a = b$$

or equally,

$$\forall a, b \in X,\ aRb \wedge a \neq b \Rightarrow \neg bRa.$$

Inequalities are _____, since for numbers a and b, a ≤ b and b ≤ a if and only if a = b. The same holds for subsets.

a. Association
b. ISAAC
c. Erlang
d. Antisymmetric

6. In functional analysis, a Banach space is called _____ if it satisfies a certain abstract property involving dual spaces. _____ spaces turn out to have desirable geometric properties.

Suppose X is a normed vector space over R or C.

a. Boolean algebra
b. Gamma test
c. Reflexive
d. Copula

7. In set theory, a binary relation can have, among other properties, _____ or irreflexivity.

At least in this context, ×X, or in other words a function from a set X into itself.

If a relation is reflexive, all elements in the set are related to themselves.

a. Completion
b. Huge
c. Double counting
d. Reflexivity

8. In mathematics, a binary relation R over a set X is transitive if whenever an element a is related to an element b, and b is in turn related to an element c, then a is also related to c.

Transitivity is a key property of both partial order relations and equivalence relations.

For example, 'is greater than,' 'is at least as great as,' and 'is equal to' are _____s:

    whenever A > B and B > C, then also A > C
    whenever A ≥ B and B ≥ C, then also A ≥ C
    whenever A = B and B = C, then also A = C

For some time, economists and philosophers believed that preference was a _____ however there are now mathematical theories which demonstrate that preferences and other significant economic results can be modelled without resorting to this assumption.

a. Directed set
b. Partial function
c. Totally ordered set
d. Transitive relation

9. In mathematics, especially order theory, a _____ formalizes the intuitive concept of an ordering, sequencing, or arrangement of the elements of a set. A poset consists of a set together with a binary relation that describes, for certain pairs of elements in the set, the requirement that one of the elements must precede the other. However, a _____ differs from a total order in that some pairs of elements may not be related to each other in this way.
a. Partially ordered set
b. Scott topology
c. Dedekind cut
d. Covering relation

10. In mathematics, given a set S, the _____ of S, written $\mathcal{P}(S)$, PS, is the set of all subsets of S. In axiomatic set theory, the existence of the _____ of any set is postulated by the axiom of _____.

Any subset F of $\mathcal{P}(S)$ is called a family of sets over S.

## Chapter 4. Relations

a. Formal power series
b. Power set
c. Polarization
d. Formal derivative

11. In mathematics and set theory, a total order, linear order, simple order, or _____
   a. Cyclic order
   b. Triadic relation
   c. Totally ordered set
   d. Linear order

12. In mathematics, especially in geometry and group theory, a _____ in $R^n$ is a discrete subgroup of $R^n$ which spans the real vector space $R^n$. Every _____ in $R^n$ can be generated from a basis for the vector space by forming all linear combinations with integral coefficients. A _____ may be viewed as a regular tiling of a space by a primitive cell.
   a. Group
   b. Lattice
   c. Boundary
   d. Homogeneity

13. A _____ is a 2D geometric symbolic representation of information according to some visualization technique. Sometimes, the technique uses a 3D visualization which is then projected onto the 2D surface. The word graph is sometimes used as a synonym for _____.
   a. 120-cell
   b. 1-center problem
   c. Diagram
   d. 2-3 heap

14. In category theory, two categories C and D are _____ if there exist functors F : C → D and G : D → C which are mutually inverse to each other. This means that both the objects and the morphisms of C and D stand in a one to one correspondence to each other. Two _____ categories share all properties that are defined solely in terms of category theory; for all practical purposes, they are identical and differ only in the notation of their objects and morphisms.
   a. Isomorphism
   b. Epimorphism
   c. Isomorphic
   d. Automorphism group

15. In mathematics, especially in order theory, the _____ of a subset S of a partially ordered set (poset) is an element of S which is greater than or equal to any other element of S. The term least element is defined dually. A bounded poset is a poset that has both a _____ and a least element.

   a. Greatest element
   b. Supremum
   c. Lower bound
   d. Majorization

16. In mathematics, especially in order theory, a _____ of a subset S of some partially ordered set is an element of S that is not smaller than any other element in S. The term minimal element is defined dually.

Let $P, \leq$ be a partially ordered set and $S \subset P$.

   a. Residuated mapping
   b. Chain complete
   c. Supremum
   d. Maximal element

17. In mathematics and logic, the phrase 'there is one and only one' is used to indicate that exactly one object with a certain property exists. In mathematical logic, this sort of quantification is known as _____ quantification or unique existential quantification.

_____ quantification is often denoted with the symbols '∃!' or '∃$_{=1}$'.

   a. A Mathematical Theory of Communication
   b. A chemical equation
   c. A posteriori
   d. Uniqueness

18. In mathematics, an _____ or member of a set is any one of the distinct objects that make up that set.

Writing A = {1,2,3,4}, means that the _____s of the set A are the numbers 1, 2, 3 and 4. Groups of _____s of A, for example {1,2}, are subsets of A.

a. Element
b. Universal code
c. Ideal
d. Order


19. The _____ problem is a fundamental problem in computational complexity theory, being a problem for which a direct proof exists that its time complexity is. In other words, an asymptotically optimal algorithm of linearithmic time complexity is known for this problem.

The general problem is stated as follows:

- Given a collection of n objects, decide whether there are any identical ones.

The algebraic decision tree model basically means that the allowable algorithms are only the ones that can perform polynomial operations of bounded degree on the input data and comparisons of the results of these computations.

Lower bounds on computational complexity of a number of algorithmic problems are proved by reducing the _____ problem to the problem in question.

a. Average cases
b. Asymptotic time complexity
c. Analyze an algorithm
d. Element uniqueness


20. In mathematics, a _____ is a statement that can be proved on the basis of explicitly stated or previously agreed assumptions.
a. Disjunction introduction
b. Boolean function
c. Logical value
d. Theorem


21. In mathematics, given a subset S of a partially ordered set T, the supremum (sup) of S, if it exists, is the least element of T that is greater than or equal to each element of S. Consequently, the supremum is also referred to as the _____, lub or _____. If the supremum exists, it may or may not belong to S.

a. Supermodular
b. Least upper bound
c. Compact element
d. Complete Heyting algebra


22. In mathematics, especially in order theory, an _____ of a subset S of some partially ordered set is an element of P which is greater than or equal to every element of S. The term lower bound is defined dually as an element of P which is lesser than or equal to every element of S. A set with an _____ is said to be bounded from above by that bound, a set with a lower bound is said to be bounded from below by that bound.
   a. Upper bound
   b. Order isomorphism
   c. Order-embedding
   d. Infinite descending chain


23. A set S of real numbers is called _____ from above if there is a real number k such that k ≥ s for all s in S. The number k is called an upper bound of S. The terms _____ from below and lower bound are similarly defined.
   a. Derivative algebra
   b. Harmonic series
   c. Descent
   d. Bounded


24. In mathematics the infimum of a subset of some set is the greatest element, not necessarily in the subset, that is less than or equal to all elements of the subset. Consequently the term _____ is also commonly used. Infima of real numbers are a common special case that is especially important in analysis.
   a. Greatest lower bound
   b. Strong antichain
   c. Strict weak ordering
   d. Supremum


25. In mathematics the _____ of a subset of some set is the greatest element, not necessarily in the subset, that is less than or equal to all elements of the subset. Consequently the term greatest lower bound is also commonly used. Infima of real numbers are a common special case that is especially important in analysis.
   a. A Mathematical Theory of Communication
   b. Infimum
   c. A chemical equation
   d. A posteriori

## Chapter 4. Relations

26. In mathematics, especially in order theory, an upper bound of a subset S of some partially ordered set is an element of P which is greater than or equal to every element of S. The term _____ is defined dually as an element of P which is lesser than or equal to every element of S. A set with an upper bound is said to be bounded from above by that bound, a set with a _____ is said to be bounded from below by that bound.
   a. Monomial order
   b. Lower bound
   c. Partially ordered set
   d. Cofinality

27. In mathematics, given a subset S of a partially ordered set T, the _____ of S, if it exists, is the least element of T that is greater than or equal to each element of S. Consequently, the _____ is also referred to as the least upper bound, lub or LUB. If the _____ exists, it may or may not belong to S.
   a. Chain complete
   b. Compact element
   c. Scott topology
   d. Supremum

28. In mathematics, an _____ is a binary relation between two elements of a set which groups them together as being 'equivalent' in some way. Let a, b, and c be arbitrary elements of some set X. Then 'a ~ b' or 'a ≡ b' denotes that a is equivalent to b.
   a. A Mathematical Theory of Communication
   b. Equivalence class
   c. Equivalence relation
   d. A chemical equation

29. In number theory, a _____ of a positive integer n is a way of writing n as a sum of positive integers. Two sums which only differ in the order of their summands are considered to be the same _____; if order matters then the sum becomes a composition. A summand in a _____ is also called a part.
   a. Distribution
   b. Derivative algebra
   c. Congruent
   d. Partition

30. In mathematics, especially in set theory, a set A is a _____ of a set B if A is 'contained' inside B. Notice that A and B may coincide. The relationship of one set being a _____ of another is called inclusion.

a. Set of all sets
b. Subset
c. Cartesian product
d. Horizontal line test

31. In mathematics, given a set X and an equivalence relation ~ on X, the _____ of an element a in X is the subset of all elements in X which are equivalent to a:

$$[a] = \{x \in X | x \sim a\}.$$

The notion of _____es is useful for constructing sets out of already constructed ones. The set of all _____es in X given an equivalence relation ~ is usually denoted as X / ~ and called the quotient set of X by ~. This operation can be thought of as the act of 'dividing' the input set by the equivalence relation, hence both the name 'quotient', and the notation, which are both reminiscent of division.

a. A Mathematical Theory of Communication
b. A chemical equation
c. Equivalence relation
d. Equivalence class

32. In set theory and its applications throughout mathematics, a _____ is a collection of sets that can be unambiguously defined by a property that all its members share. The precise definition of '_____' depends on foundational context. In work on ZF set theory, the notion of _____ is informal, whereas other set theories, such as NBG set theory, axiomatize the notion of '_____'.

a. Filter
b. Coherence
c. Congruent
d. Class

33. In geometry, a _____ is a special kind of point, usually a corner of a polygon, polyhedron, or higher dimensional polytope. In the geometry of curves a _____ is a point of where the first derivative of curvature is zero. In graph theory, a _____ is the fundamental unit out of which graphs are formed

a. Dini
b. Crib
c. Duality
d. Vertex

## Chapter 4. Relations

34. _____ is a method of mathematical proof typically used to establish that a given statement is true of all natural numbers. It is done by proving that the first statement in the infinite sequence of statements is true, and then proving that if any one statement in the infinite sequence of statements is true, then so is the next one.

The method can be extended to prove statements about more general well-founded structures, such as trees; this generalization, known as structural induction, is used in mathematical logic and computer science.

   a. Mathematical induction
   b. Herbrand structure
   c. Ground expression
   d. Finitary


35. _____ is an adjective meaning contiguous, adjoining or abutting.

In geometry, _____ is when sides meet to make an angle.

In trigonometry the _____ side of a right angled triangle is the cathetus next to the angle in question.

   a. Adjacent
   b. Ordered geometry
   c. Affine geometry
   d. Ambient space


36. In graph theory, an _____ of a vertex v in a graph is a vertex that is connected to v by an edge. The neighbourhood of a vertex v in a graph G is the induced subgraph of G consisting of all vertices adjacent to v and all edges connecting two such vertices. For example, the image shows a graph of 6 vertices and 7 edges.
   a. Adjacent vertex
   b. Articulation point
   c. Independent set
   d. Induced path


37. A _____ is one of the basic shapes of geometry: a polygon with three corners or vertices and three sides or edges which are line segments. A _____ with vertices A, B, and C is denoted ABC.

In Euclidean geometry any three non-collinear points determine a unique _____ and a unique plane.

# Chapter 4. Relations

a. Fuhrmann circle
b. Triangle
c. Kepler triangle
d. 1-center problem

38. Walking is the main form of animal locomotion on land, distinguished from running and crawling. When carried out in shallow waters, it is usually described as wading and when performed over a steeply rising object or an obstacle it becomes scrambling or climbing. The word _____ is descended from the Old English wealcan 'to roll'.
    a. 120-cell
    b. Walk
    c. 2-3 heap
    d. 1-center problem

39. In graph theory, a _____ in a graph is a sequence of vertices such that from each of its vertices there is an edge to the next vertex in the sequence. The first vertex is called the start vertex and the last vertex is called the end vertex. Both of them are called end or terminal vertices of the _____.
    a. Path
    b. Blinding
    c. Deltoid
    d. Class

40. In set theory, a _____ is a partially ordered set such that for each t ∈ T, the set {s ∈ T : s < t} is well-ordered by the relation <. For each t ∈ T, the order type of {s ∈ T : s < t} is called the height of t. The height of T itself is the least ordinal greater than the height of each element of T.
    a. Transitive reduction
    b. Definable numbers
    c. Set-theoretic topology
    d. Tree

41. In mathematical analysis, a metric space M is said to be _____ (or Cauchy) if every Cauchy sequence of points in M has a limit that is also in M or alternatively if every Cauchy sequence in M converges in M.

Intuitively, a space is _____ if there are no 'points missing' from it (inside or at the boundary.) For instance, the set of rational numbers is not _____, because $\sqrt{2}$ is 'missing' from it, even though one can construct a Cauchy sequence of rational numbers that converges to it.

a. 1-center problem
b. 120-cell
c. Complete
d. 2-3 heap


42. In the mathematical field of graph theory, a _____ is a simple graph in which every pair of distinct vertices is connected by an edge. The _____ on n vertices has n vertices and n edges, and is denoted by $K_n$. It is a regular graph of degree n − 1.
   a. 1-center problem
   b. Wheel graph
   c. 120-cell
   d. Complete graph


43. In abstract algebra, the _____, named after the ancient Greek mathematician Archimedes of Syracuse, is a property held by some groups, fields, and other algebraic structures. Roughly speaking, it is the property of having no infinitely large or infinitely small elements. This can be made precise in various contexts, for example, for fields with an absolute value, where the ordered field of real numbers is Archimedean, but the field of p-adic numbers with the p-adic absolute value is non-Archimedean.
   a. Algebraic closure
   b. Embedding problem
   c. Archimedean property
   d. Isomorphism extension theorem


44. In mathematics, a _____ is a number which can be expressed as a ratio of two integers. Non-integer _____s are usually written as the vulgar fraction $\frac{a}{b}$, where b is not zero. a is called the numerator, and b the denominator.
   a. Pre-algebra
   b. Tally marks
   c. Minkowski distance
   d. Rational number

## Chapter 5. Functions

1. The mathematical concept of a _____ expresses the intuitive idea of deterministic dependence between two quantities, one of which is viewed as primary and the other as secondary. A _____ then is a way to associate a unique output for each input of a specified type, for example, a real number or an element of a given set.
   a. Going up
   b. Grill
   c. Coherent
   d. Function

2. In mathematics, especially in the area of abstract algebra known as ring theory, a _____ is a ring with 0 ≠ 1 such that ab = 0 implies that either a = 0 or b = 0. That is, it is a nontrivial ring without left or right zero divisors. A commutative _____ is called an integral _____.
   a. Domain
   b. Left primitive ring
   c. Modular representation theory
   d. Simple ring

3. In descriptive statistics, the _____ is the length of the smallest interval which contains all the data. It is calculated by subtracting the smallest observations from the greatest and provides an indication of statistical dispersion.

   It is measured in the same units as the data.

   a. Class
   b. Bandwidth
   c. Kernel
   d. Range

4. In mathematics, an _____ is a function which associates distinct arguments with distinct values.

   An _____ is called an injection, and is also said to be an information-preserving or one-to-one function.

   A function f that is not injective is sometimes called many-to-one.

   a. Unary function
   b. A chemical equation
   c. Injective function
   d. A Mathematical Theory of Communication

5. In mathematics, a function f is said to be surjective or _____, if its values span its whole codomain; that is, for every y in the codomain, there is at least one x in the domain such that f(x) = y.

Said another way, a function f: X → Y is surjective if and only if its range f(X) is equal to its codomain Y. A surjective function is called a surjection.

a. A chemical equation
b. A posteriori
c. A Mathematical Theory of Communication
d. Onto


6. In mathematics, a function f is said to be _____ or onto, if its values span its whole codomain; that is, for every y in the codomain, there is at least one x in the domain such that f

Said another way, a function f: X → Y is _____ if and only if its range f

a. Rotation of axes
b. Linear map
c. High-dimensional model representation
d. Surjective


7. In mathematics, an _____ is a theorem with a statement beginning 'there exis ..' y, ... there exis ...'. That is, in more formal terms of symbolic logic, it is a theorem with a statement involving the existential quantifier.
a. Existence theorem
b. A chemical equation
c. A posteriori
d. A Mathematical Theory of Communication


8. In mathematics and logic, the phrase 'there is one and only one' is used to indicate that exactly one object with a certain property exists. In mathematical logic, this sort of quantification is known as _____ quantification or unique existential quantification.

_____ quantification is often denoted with the symbols '∃!' or $\exists_{=1}$'.

a. A posteriori
b. A Mathematical Theory of Communication
c. A chemical equation
d. Uniqueness

9. In mathematics, a _____ is a statement that can be proved on the basis of explicitly stated or previously agreed assumptions.
   a. Disjunction introduction
   b. Logical value
   c. Boolean function
   d. Theorem

10. In mathematics, _____ is a property that a binary operation can have. It means that, within an expression containing two or more of the same associative operators in a row, the order that the operations are performed does not matter as long as the sequence of the operands is not changed. That is, rearranging the parentheses in such an expression will not change its value.
    a. Unital
    b. Idempotence
    c. Algebraically closed
    d. Associativity

11. In mathematics, the _____ of a number n is the number that, when added to n, yields zero. The _____ of n is denoted −n. For example, 7 is −7, because 7 + (−7) = 0, and the _____ of −0.3 is 0.3, because −0.3 + 0.3 = 0.
    a. Associativity
    b. Arity
    c. Additive inverse
    d. Algebraic structure

12. An _____ is a function which does the reverse of a given function.
    a. Inverse function
    b. Empty set
    c. A Mathematical Theory of Communication
    d. Empty function

13. An _____ is an artifact, usually two-dimensional (a picture), that has a similar appearance to some subject--usually a physical object or a person.

    _____s may be two-dimensional, such as a photograph, screen display, and as well as a three-dimensional, such as a statue. They may be captured by optical devices--such as cameras, mirrors, lenses, telescopes, microscopes, etc.

a. A Mathematical Theory of Communication
b. A posteriori
c. A chemical equation
d. Image


14. In category theory, two categories C and D are _____ if there exist functors F : C → D and G : D → C which are mutually inverse to each other. This means that both the objects and the morphisms of C and D stand in a one to one correspondence to each other. Two _____ categories share all properties that are defined solely in terms of category theory; for all practical purposes, they are identical and differ only in the notation of their objects and morphisms.

   a. Epimorphism
   b. Automorphism group
   c. Isomorphic
   d. Isomorphism


15. In mathematics, an _____ in the sense of ring theory is a subring $\mathcal{O}$ of a ring R that satisfies the conditions

   1. R is a ring which is a finite-dimensional algebra over the rational number field $\mathbb{Q}$
   2. $\mathcal{O}$ spans R over $\mathbb{Q}$, so that $\mathbb{Q}\mathcal{O} = R$, and
   3. $\mathcal{O}$ is a lattice in R.

The third condition can be stated more accurately, in terms of the extension of scalars of R to the real numbers, embedding R in a real vector space. In less formal terms, additively $\mathcal{O}$ should be a free abelian group generated by a basis for R over $\mathbb{Q}$.

The leading example is the case where R is a number field K and $\mathcal{O}$ is its ring of integers. In algebraic number theory there are examples for any K other than the rational field of proper subrings of the ring of integers that are also _____s.

   a. Algebraic
   b. Annihilator
   c. Efficiency
   d. Order


16. In the mathematical field of order theory an _____ is a special kind of monotone function that constitutes a suitable notion of isomorphism for partially ordered sets. Whenever two posets are order isomorphic, they can be considered to be 'essentially the same' in the sense that one of the orders can be obtained from the other just by renaming of elements. Two strictly weaker notions that relate to _____s are order embeddings and Galois connections.

a. Infinite descending chain
b. Order isomorphism
c. Upper bound
d. Infima

17. In abstract algebra, an _____ is a bijective map f such that both f and its inverse $f^{-1}$ are homomorphisms.

In the more general setting of category theory, an _____ is a morphism f:X→Y in a category for which there exists an 'inverse' $f^{-1}$:Y→X, with the property that both $f^{-1}f=id_X$ and $ff^{-1}=id_Y$.

Informally, an _____ is a kind of mapping between objects, which shows a relationship between two properties or operations.

a. Epimorphism
b. Automorphism group
c. Isomorphic
d. Isomorphism

18. Leonardo of Pisa (c. 1170 - c. 1250), also known as Leonardo Pisano, Leonardo Bonacci, Leonardo _____, or, most commonly, simply _____, was an Italian mathematician, considered by some 'the most talented mathematician of the Middle Ages'.
a. Guido Castelnuovo
b. Harry Hinsley
c. Ralph C. Merkle
d. Fibonacci

19. In mathematics, _____ and undefined are used to explain whether or not expressions have meaningful, sensible, and unambiguous values. Not all branches of mathematics come to the same conclusion.

The following expressions are undefined in all contexts, but remarks in the analysis section may apply.

a. Toy model
b. Defined
c. LHS
d. Plugging in

## Chapter 5. Functions

20. A set S of real numbers is called _____ from above if there is a real number k such that k ≥ s for all s in S. The number k is called an upper bound of S. The terms _____ from below and lower bound are similarly defined.
    a. Bounded
    b. Descent
    c. Harmonic series
    d. Derivative algebra

21. An important special case is a _____, where X is taken to be the set N of natural numbers. Thus a sequence f = ( $a_0$, $a_1$, $a_2$, ... ) is bounded if there exists a number M > 0 such that

    $|a_n| \leq M$

    for every natural number n.

    a. 120-cell
    b. 2-3 heap
    c. 1-center problem
    d. Bounded Sequence

22. In calculus, a function f defined on a subset of the real numbers with real values is called monotonic (also monotonically increasing or non-_____), if for all x and y such that x ≤ y one has f(x) ≤ f(y), so f preserves the order. In layman's terms, the sign of the slope is always positive (the curve tending upwards) or zero (i.e., non-_____, or asymptotic, or depicted as a horizontal, flat line) Likewise, a function is called monotonically _____ (non-increasing) if, whenever x ≤ y, then f(x) ≥ f(y), so it reverses the order.
    a. Tensor product of Hilbert spaces
    b. Decreasing
    c. Circular convolution
    d. Dual pair

23. In mathematics, a _____ function is a function which preserves the given order. This concept first arose in calculus, and was later generalized to the more abstract setting of order theory.

In calculus, a function f defined on a subset of the real numbers with real values is called _____, if for all x and y such that x ≤ y one has f≤ f

a. Monotonic
b. Compact convergence
c. $C_0$-semigroup
d. Negacyclic convolution

24. In mathematics, a _____ of some sequence is a new sequence which is formed from the original sequence by deleting some of the elements without disturbing the relative positions of the remaining elements.

Formally, suppose that X is a set and that $_{k \in K}$ is a sequence in X, where K = {1,2,3,...,n} if is a finite sequence and K = N if is an infinite sequence. Then, a _____ of is a sequence of the form $(a_{n_r})$ where is a strictly increasing sequence in the index set K.

a. Subsequence
b. Cognitively Guided Instruction
c. Nicomachus's theorem
d. Point plotting

25. In mathematics, a _____ is a calculation involving two operands, in other words, an operation whose arity is two. _____s can be accomplished using either a binary function or binary operator. _____s are sometimes called dyadic operations in order to avoid confusion with the binary numeral system.
a. 2-3 heap
b. 1-center problem
c. Binary operation
d. 120-cell

26. In linear algebra and functional analysis, a _____ is a linear transformation P from a vector space to itself such that $P^2 = P$. It leaves its image unchanged. Though abstract, this definition of '_____' formalizes and generalizes the idea of graphical _____.
a. Characteristic function
b. Deviance
c. Critical point
d. Projection

27. In abstract algebra, a _____ or Boolean lattice is a complemented distributive lattice. This type of algebraic structure captures essential properties of both set operations and logic operations. A _____ can be seen as a generalization of a power set algebra or a field of sets.

a. Duality
b. Boolean algebra
c. Figure-eight knot
d. Filter

28. In mathematics, the term _____ has several different important meanings:

   - An _____ is an equality that remains true regardless of the values of any variables that appear within it, to distinguish it from an equality which is true under more particular conditions. For this, the 'triple bar' symbol ≡ is sometimes used.
   - In algebra, an _____ or _____ element of a set S with a binary operation Â· is an element e that, when combined with any element x of S, produces that same x. That is, eÂ·x = xÂ·e = x for all x in S.
     - The _____ function from a set S to itself, often denoted id or id$_S$, s the function such that i = x for all x in S. This function serves as the _____ element in the set of all functions from S to itself with respect to function composition.
     - In linear algebra, the _____ matrix of size n is the n-by-n square matrix with ones on the main diagonal and zeros elsewhere. This matrix serves as the _____ with respect to matrix multiplication.

A common example of the first meaning is the trigonometric _____

$$\sin^2 \theta + \cos^2 \theta = 1$$

which is true for all real values of θ, as opposed to

$$\cos \theta = 1,$$

which is true only for some values of θ, not all. For example, the latter equation is true when $\theta = 0$, false when $\theta = 2$

The concepts of 'additive _____' and 'multiplicative _____' are central to the Peano axioms. The number 0 is the 'additive _____' for integers, real numbers, and complex numbers. For the real numbers, for all $a \in \mathbb{R}$,

$$0 + a = a,$$

$$a + 0 = a, \text{ and}$$

$$0 + 0 = 0.$$

Similarly, The number 1 is the 'multiplicative _____' for integers, real numbers, and complex numbers.

a. Action
b. Intersection
c. ARIA
d. Identity

29. In mathematics, a _____ is an operation with only one operand.

Common notations are prefix notation, postfix notation, and functional notation. In the case of the square root a horizontal bar over the argument extending the square root sign can indicate the extent of the argument, so that parentheses can be dispensed with.

a. A chemical equation
b. Unary operation
c. Identity
d. A Mathematical Theory of Communication

## Chapter 6. Elementary Number Theory

1. _____ is the branch of pure mathematics concerned with the properties of numbers in general, and integers in particular, as well as the wider classes of problems that arise from their study.

   _____ may be subdivided into several fields, according to the methods used and the type of questions investigated.

   The term 'arithmetic' is also used to refer to _____.

   a. Number theory
   b. Sociable number
   c. Coin problem
   d. Goormaghtigh conjecture


2. In mathematics, a _____ is a natural number which has exactly two distinct natural number divisors: 1 and itself. An infinitude of _____s exists, as demonstrated by Euclid around 300 BC. The first twenty-five _____s are:

   2, 3, 5, 7, 11, 13, 17, 19, 23, 29, 31, 37, 41, 43, 47, 53, 59, 61, 67, 71, 73, 79, 83, 89, 97.

   a. Perrin number
   b. Pronic number
   c. Highly composite number
   d. Prime number


3. The word _____ has many distinct meanings in different fields of knowledge, depending on their methodologies and the context of discussion. Broadly speaking we can say that a _____ is some kind of belief or claim that (supposedly) explains, asserts, or consolidates some class of claims. Additionally, in contrast with a theorem the statement of the _____ is generally accepted only in some tentative fashion as opposed to regarding it as having been conclusively established.
   a. Per mil
   b. Theory
   c. Defined
   d. Transport of structure


4. In mathematics, _____ is a property that a binary operation can have. It means that, within an expression containing two or more of the same associative operators in a row, the order that the operations are performed does not matter as long as the sequence of the operands is not changed. That is, rearranging the parentheses in such an expression will not change its value.

a. Algebraically closed
b. Unital
c. Associativity
d. Idempotence

5. In mathematics, a _____ is a calculation involving two operands, in other words, an operation whose arity is two. _____s can be accomplished using either a binary function or binary operator. _____s are sometimes called dyadic operations in order to avoid confusion with the binary numeral system.
  a. 2-3 heap
  b. 120-cell
  c. 1-center problem
  d. Binary operation

6. _____ is a method of mathematical proof typically used to establish that a given statement is true of all natural numbers. It is done by proving that the first statement in the infinite sequence of statements is true, and then proving that if any one statement in the infinite sequence of statements is true, then so is the next one.

The method can be extended to prove statements about more general well-founded structures, such as trees; this generalization, known as structural induction, is used in mathematical logic and computer science.

  a. Ground expression
  b. Mathematical induction
  c. Herbrand structure
  d. Finitary

7. In mathematics and set theory, a total order, linear order, simple order, or
  a. Linear order
  b. Triadic relation
  c. Cyclic order
  d. Totally ordered set

8. In quantum field theory and statistical mechanics in the thermodynamic limit, a system with a global symmetry can have more than one phase. For parameters where the symmetry is spontaneously broken, the system is said to be _____. When the global symmetry is unbroken the system is disordered.

## Chapter 6. Elementary Number Theory

a. Ordered
b. Isoenthalpic-isobaric ensemble
c. Einstein relation
d. Ursell function

9. In mathematics, an _____ is a theorem with a statement beginning 'there exis ..' y, ... there exis ...'. That is, in more formal terms of symbolic logic, it is a theorem with a statement involving the existential quantifier.
   a. A posteriori
   b. Existence theorem
   c. A chemical equation
   d. A Mathematical Theory of Communication

10. In mathematics and logic, the phrase 'there is one and only one' is used to indicate that exactly one object with a certain property exists. In mathematical logic, this sort of quantification is known as _____ quantification or unique existential quantification.

    _____ quantification is often denoted with the symbols '∃!' or $\exists_{=1}$'.

    a. A posteriori
    b. A Mathematical Theory of Communication
    c. A chemical equation
    d. Uniqueness

11. In mathematics, computing, linguistics and related subjects, an _____ is a sequence of finite instructions, often used for calculation and data processing. It is formally a type of effective method in which a list of well-defined instructions for completing a task will, when given an initial state, proceed through a well-defined series of successive states, eventually terminating in an end-state. The transition from one state to the next is not necessarily deterministic; some _____s, known as probabilistic _____s, incorporate randomness.
    a. In-place algorithm
    b. Out-of-core
    c. Approximate counting algorithm
    d. Algorithm

12. In mathematics, a _____ is a statement that can be proved on the basis of explicitly stated or previously agreed assumptions.

## Chapter 6. Elementary Number Theory

a. Boolean function
b. Logical value
c. Disjunction introduction
d. Theorem

13. A _____ number is a positive integer which has a positive divisor other than one or itself. By definition, every integer greater than one is either a prime number or a _____ number. zero and one are considered to be neither prime nor _____. For example, the integer 14 is a _____ number because it can be factored as 2 × 7.
    a. Key server
    b. Basis
    c. Discontinuity
    d. Composite

14. A _____ is a positive integer which has a positive divisor other than one or itself. In other words, if 0 < n is an integer and there are integers 1 < a, b < n such that n = a × b then n is composite. By definition, every integer greater than one is either a prime number or a _____.
    a. Composite number
    b. Ruth-Aaron pair
    c. Prime Pages
    d. Megaprime

15. In number theory, the _____ is an algorithm to determine the greatest common divisor of two elements of any Euclidean domain. Its major significance is that it does not require factoring the two integers, and it is also significant in that it is one of the oldest algorithms known, dating back to the ancient Greeks.

    The _____ is one of the oldest algorithms known, since it appeared in Euclid's Elements around 300 BC.

    a. A chemical equation
    b. A posteriori
    c. A Mathematical Theory of Communication
    d. Euclidean algorithm

## Chapter 6. Elementary Number Theory

16. In mathematics, an _____ in the sense of ring theory is a subring $\mathcal{O}$ of a ring R that satisfies the conditions

    1. R is a ring which is a finite-dimensional algebra over the rational number field $\mathbb{Q}$
    2. $\mathcal{O}$ spans R over $\mathbb{Q}$, so that $\mathbb{Q}\mathcal{O} = R$, and
    3. $\mathcal{O}$ is a lattice in R.

The third condition can be stated more accurately, in terms of the extension of scalars of R to the real numbers, embedding R in a real vector space. In less formal terms, additively $\mathcal{O}$ should be a free abelian group generated by a basis for R over $\mathbb{Q}$.

The leading example is the case where R is a number field K and $\mathcal{O}$ is its ring of integers. In algebraic number theory there are examples for any K other than the rational field of proper subrings of the ring of integers that are also _____s.

   a. Algebraic
   b. Efficiency
   c. Annihilator
   d. Order


17. In mathematics, the _____, sometimes known as the greatest common factor or highest common factor, of two non-zero integers, is the largest positive integer that divides both numbers without remainder.

This notion can be extended to polynomials, see _____ of two polynomials.

The _____ of a and b is written as gc, or sometimes simply as.

   a. Multiplication
   b. Highest common factor
   c. Minuend
   d. Greatest common divisor


18. In arithmetic and number theory, the _____ or lowest common multiple or smallest common multiple of two integers a and b is the smallest positive integer that is a multiple of both a and b. Since it is a multiple, it can be divided by a and b without a remainder. If either a or b is 0, so that there is no such positive integer, then lc is defined to be zero.

   a. Least common multiple
   b. Lowest common denominator
   c. Plus-minus sign
   d. Plus and minus signs

## Chapter 6. Elementary Number Theory

19. In mathematics, a _____ of an integer n is an integer which evenly divides n without leaving a remainder.

For example, 7 is a _____ of 42 because 42/7 = 6. We also say 42 is divisible by 7 or 42 is a multiple of 7 or 7 divides 42 or 7 is a factor of 42 and we usually write 7 | 42.

a. 2-3 heap
b. 120-cell
c. 1-center problem
d. Divisor

20. In combinatorial mathematics, a _____ is an un-ordered collection of distinct elements, usually of a prescribed size and taken from a given set. Given such a set S, a _____ of elements of S is just a subset of S, where as always forsets the order of the elements is not taken into account. Also, as always forsets, no elements can be repeated more than once in a _____; this is often referred to as a 'collection without repetition'.

a. Fill-in
b. Heawood number
c. Sparsity
d. Combination

21. In mathematics, _____ are a concept central to linear algebra and related fields of mathematics

Suppose that K is a field and V is a vector space over K.

a. Setoid
b. Linear span
c. Polarization
d. Linear combinations

22. In number theory, the _____ states that every natural number greater than 1 can be written as a unique product of prime numbers. For instance,

$$6936 = 2^3 \times 3 \times 17^2,$$

$$1200 = 2^4 \times 3 \times 5^2.$$

There are no other possible factorizations of 6936 or 1200 into non-negative prime numbers. The above representation collapses repeated prime factors into powers for easier identification.

a. Fundamental theorem of arithmetic
b. Dedekind sums
c. Cyclic number
d. Feit–Thompson theorem



23. As an abstract term, _____ means similarity between objects.
a. 1-center problem
b. 2-3 heap
c. 120-cell
d. Congruence



24. The word _____ is the Latin ablative of modulus which itself means 'a small measure.' It was introduced into mathematics in the book Disquisitiones Arithmeticae by Carl Friedrich Gauss in 1801. Ever since, however, '_____' has gained many meanings, some exact and some imprecise.

- (This usage is from Gauss's book.) Given the integers a, b and n, the expression a ≡ b (mod n) means that a − b is a multiple of n, or equivalently, a and b both leave the same remainder when divided by n. For more details, see modular arithmetic.

- In computing, given two numbers (either integer or real), a and n, a _____ n is the remainder after numerical division of a by n, under certain constraints. See _____ operation.

a. Per mil
b. Predictor-corrector method
c. Quotition
d. Modulo



25. In mathematics, given a set X and an equivalence relation ~ on X, the _____ of an element a in X is the subset of all elements in X which are equivalent to a:

$$[a] = \{x \in X | x \sim a\}.$$

The notion of _____ es is useful for constructing sets out of already constructed ones. The set of all _____ es in X given an equivalence relation ~ is usually denoted as X / ~ and called the quotient set of X by ~. This operation can be thought of as the act of 'dividing' the input set by the equivalence relation, hence both the name 'quotient', and the notation, which are both reminiscent of division.

## Chapter 6. Elementary Number Theory

a. A Mathematical Theory of Communication
b. A chemical equation
c. Equivalence relation
d. Equivalence class

26. In the study of metric spaces in mathematics, there are various notions of two metrics on the same underlying space being 'the same', or _____.

In the following, M will denote a non-empty set and $d_1$ and $d_2$ will denote two metrics on M.

The two metrics $d_1$ and $d_2$ are said to be topologically _____ if they generate the same topology on M.

a. Equivalent
b. A Mathematical Theory of Communication
c. A posteriori
d. A chemical equation

27. The _____ are the set of numbers consisting of the natural numbers including 0 and their negatives. They are numbers that can be written without a fractional or decimal component, and fall within the set {... −2, −1, 0, 1, 2, ...}.

a. A Mathematical Theory of Communication
b. A posteriori
c. A chemical equation
d. Integers

28. In number theory, a _____ of a positive integer n is a way of writing n as a sum of positive integers. Two sums which only differ in the order of their summands are considered to be the same _____; if order matters then the sum becomes a composition. A summand in a _____ is also called a part.

a. Derivative algebra
b. Congruent
c. Distribution
d. Partition

29. In set theory and its applications throughout mathematics, a _____ is a collection of sets that can be unambiguously defined by a property that all its members share. The precise definition of '_____' depends on foundational context. In work on ZF set theory, the notion of _____ is informal, whereas other set theories, such as NBG set theory, axiomatize the notion of '_____'.

## Chapter 6. Elementary Number Theory

a. Filter
b. Coherence
c. Congruent
d. Class

30. _____ is the mathematical operation of scaling one number by another. It is one of the four basic operations in elementary arithmetic.

_____ is defined for whole numbers in terms of repeated addition; for example, 4 multiplied by 3 can be calculated by adding 3 copies of 4 together:

$$4 + 4 + 4 = 12.$$

_____ of rational numbers and real numbers is defined by systematic generalization of this basic idea.

a. Highest common factor
b. The number 0 is even.
c. Least common multiple
d. Multiplication

31. In mathematical analysis, a metric space M is said to be _____ (or Cauchy) if every Cauchy sequence of points in M has a limit that is also in M or alternatively if every Cauchy sequence in M converges in M.

Intuitively, a space is _____ if there are no 'points missing' from it (inside or at the boundary.) For instance, the set of rational numbers is not _____, because $\sqrt{2}$ is 'missing' from it, even though one can construct a Cauchy sequence of rational numbers that converges to it.

a. 2-3 heap
b. 1-center problem
c. Complete
d. 120-cell

32. In mathematics, the term _____ is used to specify that a certain concept or object (a function, a property, a relation, etc.) is defined in a mathematical or logical way using a set of base axioms in an entirely unambiguous way and satisfies the properties it is required to satisfy. Usually definitions are stated unambiguously, and it is clear they satisfy the required properties.

a. Defined
b. Quotition
c. Handwaving
d. Well-defined

33. In mathematics, the _____ of a number n is the number that, when added to n, yields zero. The _____ of n is denoted −n. For example, 7 is −7, because 7 + (−7) = 0, and the _____ of −0.3 is 0.3, because −0.3 + 0.3 = 0.
    a. Associativity
    b. Algebraic structure
    c. Arity
    d. Additive inverse

34. In mathematics, a _____ for a number x, denoted by $1/x$ or $x^{-1}$, is a number which when multiplied by x yields the multiplicative identity, 1. The _____ of x is also called the reciprocal of x. The _____ of a fraction $p/q$ is $q/p$.
    a. Golden function
    b. Hyperbolic function
    c. Double exponential
    d. Multiplicative inverse

35. In mathematics, an _____ is a binary relation between two elements of a set which groups them together as being 'equivalent' in some way. Let a, b, and c be arbitrary elements of some set X. Then 'a ~ b' or 'a ≡ b' denotes that a is equivalent to b.
    a. Equivalence class
    b. A Mathematical Theory of Communication
    c. A chemical equation
    d. Equivalence relation

## Chapter 7. Cardinality

1. _____ Galilei (15 February 1564 - 8 January 1642) was a Tuscan physicist, mathematician, astronomer, and philosopher who played a major role in the Scientific Revolution. His achievements include improvements to the telescope and consequent astronomical observations, and support for Copernicanism. _____ has been called the 'father of modern observational astronomy', the 'father of modern physics', the 'father of science', and 'the Father of Modern Science.' The motion of uniformly accelerated objects, taught in nearly all high school and introductory college physics courses, was studied by _____ as the subject of kinematics.
    a. David Naccache
    b. Francesco Severi
    c. Galileo
    d. Jan Kowalewski

2. In mathematics, the _____ of a set is a measure of the 'number of elements of the set'. For example, the set A = {1, 2, 3} contains 3 elements, and therefore A has a _____ of 3. There are two approaches to _____ - one which compares sets directly using bijections and injections, and another which uses cardinal numbers.
    a. 2-3 heap
    b. 120-cell
    c. 1-center problem
    d. Cardinality

3. In mathematics, an _____ is a binary relation between two elements of a set which groups them together as being 'equivalent' in some way. Let a, b, and c be arbitrary elements of some set X. Then 'a ~ b' or 'a ≡ b' denotes that a is equivalent to b.
    a. Equivalence relation
    b. A chemical equation
    c. Equivalence class
    d. A Mathematical Theory of Communication

4. In mathematics, especially in the area of abstract algebra known as ring theory, a _____ is a ring with 0 ≠ 1 such that ab = 0 implies that either a = 0 or b = 0. That is, it is a nontrivial ring without left or right zero divisors. A commutative _____ is called an integral _____.
    a. Modular representation theory
    b. Domain
    c. Left primitive ring
    d. Simple ring

5. _____ is a process of conveying information about characters in fiction or conversation. Characters are usually present by description and through their actions, speech, and thoughts.

At performance an actor has less time to characterize and so can risk the character coming across as underdeveloped.

a. 1-center problem
b. 2-3 heap
c. 120-cell
d. Characterization


6. In mathematics, a _____ is a set with the same cardinality as some subset of the set of natural numbers. The term was originated by Georg Cantor; it stems from the fact that the natural numbers are often called counting numbers. A set that is not countable is called uncountable.

a. Transfinite numbers
b. Countable set
c. Dedekind-infinite
d. Cofinite


7. In mathematics, a _____ is a number which can be expressed as a ratio of two integers. Non-integer _____s are usually written as the vulgar fraction $\frac{a}{b}$, where b is not zero. a is called the numerator, and b the denominator.

a. Pre-algebra
b. Rational number
c. Minkowski distance
d. Tally marks


8. _____ is a method of mathematical proof typically used to establish that a given statement is true of all natural numbers. It is done by proving that the first statement in the infinite sequence of statements is true, and then proving that if any one statement in the infinite sequence of statements is true, then so is the next one.

The method can be extended to prove statements about more general well-founded structures, such as trees; this generalization, known as structural induction, is used in mathematical logic and computer science.

a. Mathematical induction
b. Herbrand structure
c. Finitary
d. Ground expression

## Chapter 7. Cardinality

9. In mathematics, given a set S, the _____ of S, written $\mathcal{P}(S)$, PS, is the set of all subsets of S. In axiomatic set theory, the existence of the _____ of any set is postulated by the axiom of _____.

Any subset F of $\mathcal{P}(S)$ is called a family of sets over S.

   a. Formal power series
   b. Formal derivative
   c. Polarization
   d. Power set

10. In mathematics, an _____ is an infinite set which is too big to be countable. The uncountability of a set is closely related to its cardinal number: a set is uncountable if its cardinal number is larger than that of the natural numbers. The related term nondenumerable set is used by some authors as a synonym for '_____' while other authors define a set to be nondenumerable if it is not an infinite countable set.

   a. Uncountable set
   b. A posteriori
   c. A Mathematical Theory of Communication
   d. A chemical equation

11. In set theory, the term _____ refers to a set operation used in the convergence of set elements to form a resultant set containing the elements of both sets. As a simple example, a _____ of two disjoint sets, which do not have elements in common results in a set containing all elements from both sets. A Venn diagram representing the _____ of sets A and B.

   a. Event
   b. Introduction
   c. UES
   d. Union

12. In abstract algebra, the _____, named after the ancient Greek mathematician Archimedes of Syracuse, is a property held by some groups, fields, and other algebraic structures. Roughly speaking, it is the property of having no infinitely large or infinitely small elements. This can be made precise in various contexts, for example, for fields with an absolute value, where the ordered field of real numbers is Archimedean, but the field of p-adic numbers with the p-adic absolute value is non-Archimedean.

   a. Isomorphism extension theorem
   b. Embedding problem
   c. Archimedean property
   d. Algebraic closure

## Chapter 7. Cardinality

13. In mathematics, the _____ of a ring R, often denoted cha, is defined to be the smallest number of times one must add the ring's multiplicative identity element to itself to get the additive identity element; the ring is said to have _____ zero if this repeated sum never reaches the additive identity. That is, cha is the smallest positive number n such that

$$\underbrace{1 + \cdots + 1}_{n \text{ summands}} = 0$$

if such a number n exists, and 0 otherwise. The _____ may also be taken to be the exponent of the ring's additive group, that is, the smallest positive n such that

$$\underbrace{a + \cdots + a}_{n \text{ summands}} = 0$$

for every element a of the ring.

   a. Disk
   b. Coherent
   c. Characteristic
   d. Class


14. In probability theory, the _____ of any random variable completely defines its probability distribution. On the real line it is given by the following formula, where X is any random variable with the distribution in question:

$$\varphi_X(t) = \mathrm{E}\left(e^{itX}\right)$$

where t is a real number, i is the imaginary unit, and E denotes the expected value.

If $F_X$ is the cumulative distribution function, then the _____ is given by the Riemann-Stieltjes integral

$$\mathrm{E}\left(e^{itX}\right) = \int_{-\infty}^{\infty} e^{itx} \, dF_X(x).$$

In cases in which there is a probability density function, $f_X$, this becomes

$$\mathrm{E}\left(e^{itX}\right) = \int_{-\infty}^{\infty} e^{itx} f_X(x) \, dx.$$

If X is a vector-valued random variable, one takes the argument t to be a vector and tX to be a dot product.

a. Class
b. Censoring
c. Boussinesq approximation
d. Characteristic function

15. The mathematical concept of a _____ expresses the intuitive idea of deterministic dependence between two quantities, one of which is viewed as primary and the other as secondary. A _____ then is a way to associate a unique output for each input of a specified type, for example, a real number or an element of a given set.

   a. Going up
   b. Coherent
   c. Grill
   d. Function

16. In mathematics, given a set X and an equivalence relation ~ on X, the _____ of an element a in X is the subset of all elements in X which are equivalent to a:

$$[a] = \{x \in X | x \sim a\}.$$

The notion of _____es is useful for constructing sets out of already constructed ones. The set of all _____es in X given an equivalence relation ~ is usually denoted as X / ~ and called the quotient set of X by ~. This operation can be thought of as the act of 'dividing' the input set by the equivalence relation, hence both the name 'quotient', and the notation, which are both reminiscent of division.

   a. A chemical equation
   b. A Mathematical Theory of Communication
   c. Equivalence relation
   d. Equivalence class

17. In set theory and its applications throughout mathematics, a _____ is a collection of sets that can be unambiguously defined by a property that all its members share. The precise definition of '_____' depends on foundational context. In work on ZF set theory, the notion of _____ is informal, whereas other set theories, such as NBG set theory, axiomatize the notion of '_____'.

   a. Filter
   b. Coherence
   c. Congruent
   d. Class

18. In mathematics, a binary relation R on a set X is _____ if, for all a and b in X, if a is R to b and b is R to a, then a = b.

In mathematical notation, this is:

$$\forall a, b \in X, \ aRb \land bRa \Rightarrow a = b$$

or equally,

$$\forall a, b \in X, \ aRb \land a \neq b \Rightarrow \neg bRa.$$

Inequalities are _____, since for numbers a and b, a ≤ b and b ≤ a if and only if a = b. The same holds for subsets.

   a. Antisymmetric
   b. Association
   c. Erlang
   d. ISAAC


19. In functional analysis, a Banach space is called _____ if it satisfies a certain abstract property involving dual spaces. _____ spaces turn out to have desirable geometric properties.

Suppose X is a normed vector space over R or C.

   a. Copula
   b. Gamma test
   c. Boolean algebra
   d. Reflexive


20. In set theory, a binary relation can have, among other properties, _____ or irreflexivity.

At least in this context, ×X, or in other words a function from a set X into itself.

If a relation is reflexive, all elements in the set are related to themselves.

   a. Double counting
   b. Huge
   c. Completion
   d. Reflexivity

## Chapter 7. Cardinality

21. In mathematics, a binary relation R over a set X is transitive if whenever an element a is related to an element b, and b is in turn related to an element c, then a is also related to c.

Transitivity is a key property of both partial order relations and equivalence relations.

For example, 'is greater than,' 'is at least as great as,' and 'is equal to' are _____s:

    whenever A > B and B > C, then also A > C
    whenever A ≥ B and B ≥ C, then also A ≥ C
    whenever A = B and B = C, then also A = C

For some time, economists and philosophers believed that preference was a _____ however there are now mathematical theories which demonstrate that preferences and other significant economic results can be modelled without resorting to this assumption.

  a. Totally ordered set
  b. Partial function
  c. Directed set
  d. Transitive relation


22. In mathematics, a _____ is a statement that can be proved on the basis of explicitly stated or previously agreed assumptions.
  a. Disjunction introduction
  b. Logical value
  c. Theorem
  d. Boolean function


23. In number theory, a _____ of a positive integer n is a way of writing n as a sum of positive integers. Two sums which only differ in the order of their summands are considered to be the same _____; if order matters then the sum becomes a composition. A summand in a _____ is also called a part.
  a. Partition
  b. Distribution
  c. Congruent
  d. Derivative algebra


24. In mathematics and set theory, a total order, linear order, simple order, or

a. Triadic relation
b. Linear order
c. Totally ordered set
d. Cyclic order

25. In quantum field theory and statistical mechanics in the thermodynamic limit, a system with a global symmetry can have more than one phase. For parameters where the symmetry is spontaneously broken, the system is said to be _____. When the global symmetry is unbroken the system is disordered.
    a. Isoenthalpic-isobaric ensemble
    b. Ursell function
    c. Einstein relation
    d. Ordered

26. In mathematics, the word _____ has at least two distinct meanings, outlined in the sections below. For other uses see _____.

The term the _____ sometimes denotes the real line.

   a. Christofides heuristics algorithm
   b. Continuum
   c. Barrelled spaces
   d. Coordinate rotations and reflections

27. In mathematics, the _____ is a hypothesis, advanced by Georg Cantor, about the possible sizes of infinite sets. Cantor introduced the concept of cardinality to compare the sizes of infinite sets, and he gave two proofs that the cardinality of the set of integers is strictly smaller than that of the set of real numbers. His proofs, however, give no indication of the extent to which the cardinality of the natural numbers is less than that of the real numbers.
    a. Continuum hypothesis
    b. Blotto game
    c. Closed under some operation
    d. Compact groups

*Chapter 7. Cardinality*  55

28. In mathematics, an _____ in the sense of ring theory is a subring $\mathcal{O}$ of a ring R that satisfies the conditions

   1. R is a ring which is a finite-dimensional algebra over the rational number field $\mathbb{Q}$
   2. $\mathcal{O}$ spans R over $\mathbb{Q}$, so that $\mathbb{Q}\mathcal{O} = R$, and
   3. $\mathcal{O}$ is a lattice in R.

The third condition can be stated more accurately, in terms of the extension of scalars of R to the real numbers, embedding R in a real vector space. In less formal terms, additively $\mathcal{O}$ should be a free abelian group generated by a basis for R over $\mathbb{Q}$.

The leading example is the case where R is a number field K and $\mathcal{O}$ is its ring of integers. In algebraic number theory there are examples for any K other than the rational field of proper subrings of the ring of integers that are also _____s.

   a. Order
   b. Algebraic
   c. Efficiency
   d. Annihilator


29. In the mathematical field of order theory an _____ is a special kind of monotone function that constitutes a suitable notion of isomorphism for partially ordered sets. Whenever two posets are order isomorphic, they can be considered to be 'essentially the same' in the sense that one of the orders can be obtained from the other just by renaming of elements. Two strictly weaker notions that relate to _____s are order embeddings and Galois connections.

   a. Infima
   b. Upper bound
   c. Infinite descending chain
   d. Order isomorphism


30. In abstract algebra, an _____ is a bijective map f such that both f and its inverse $f^{-1}$ are homomorphisms.

In the more general setting of category theory, an _____ is a morphism f:X→Y in a category for which there exists an 'inverse' $f^{-1}$:Y→X, with the property that both $f^{-1}f=id_X$ and $ff^{-1}=id_Y$.

Informally, an _____ is a kind of mapping between objects, which shows a relationship between two properties or operations.

a. Epimorphism
b. Isomorphism
c. Isomorphic
d. Automorphism group

## Chapter 8. The Real Numbers

1. In mathematics, the _____ of a number n is the number that, when added to n, yields zero. The _____ of n is denoted −n. For example, 7 is −7, because 7 + (−7) = 0, and the _____ of −0.3 is 0.3, because −0.3 + 0.3 = 0.
   a. Associativity
   b. Additive inverse
   c. Algebraic structure
   d. Arity

2. In traditional logic, an _____ or postulate is a proposition that is not proved or demonstrated but considered to be either self-evident, or subject to necessary decision. Therefore, its truth is taken for granted, and serves as a starting point for deducing and inferring other truths.

   In mathematics, the term _____ is used in two related but distinguishable senses: 'logical _____s' and 'non-logical _____s'.

   a. Enumerative definition
   b. AND-OR-Invert
   c. Algebraic logic
   d. Axiom

3. In mathematics, a _____ for a number x, denoted by $1/x$ or $x^{-1}$, is a number which when multiplied by x yields the multiplicative identity, 1. The _____ of x is also called the reciprocal of x. The _____ of a fraction $p/q$ is $q/p$.
   a. Golden function
   b. Double exponential
   c. Hyperbolic function
   d. Multiplicative inverse

4. In mathematics, the _____s may be described informally in several different ways. The _____s include both rational numbers, such as 42 and −23/129, and irrational numbers, such as pi and the square root of two; or, a _____ can be given by an infinite decimal representation, such as 2.4871773339...., where the digits continue in some way; or, the _____s may be thought of as points on an infinitely long number line.

   These descriptions of the _____s, while intuitively accessible, are not sufficiently rigorous for the purposes of pure mathematics.

   a. Pre-algebra
   b. Tally marks
   c. Minkowski distance
   d. Real number

5. In abstract algebra, the _____, named after the ancient Greek mathematician Archimedes of Syracuse, is a property held by some groups, fields, and other algebraic structures. Roughly speaking, it is the property of having no infinitely large or infinitely small elements. This can be made precise in various contexts, for example, for fields with an absolute value, where the ordered field of real numbers is Archimedean, but the field of p-adic numbers with the p-adic absolute value is non-Archimedean.
   a. Embedding problem
   b. Algebraic closure
   c. Isomorphism extension theorem
   d. Archimedean property

6. In mathematics, _____ is a property that a binary operation can have. It means that, within an expression containing two or more of the same associative operators in a row, the order that the operations are performed does not matter as long as the sequence of the operands is not changed. That is, rearranging the parentheses in such an expression will not change its value.
   a. Associativity
   b. Algebraically closed
   c. Unital
   d. Idempotence

7. In mathematics, a _____ is a calculation involving two operands, in other words, an operation whose arity is two. _____s can be accomplished using either a binary function or binary operator. _____s are sometimes called dyadic operations in order to avoid confusion with the binary numeral system.
   a. 120-cell
   b. 2-3 heap
   c. 1-center problem
   d. Binary operation

8. In abstract algebra, a _____ is an algebraic structure in which the operations of addition, subtraction, multiplication and division may be performed in a way that satisfies some familiar rules from the arithmetic of ordinary numbers.

All _____s are rings, but not conversely. _____s differ from rings most importantly in the requirement that division be possible, but also, in modern definitions, by the requirement that the multiplication operation in a _____ be commutative.

   a. Chord
   b. Functional
   c. Blind
   d. Field

9. In mathematics, the term _____ has several different important meanings:

- An _____ is an equality that remains true regardless of the values of any variables that appear within it, to distinguish it from an equality which is true under more particular conditions. For this, the 'triple bar' symbol ≡ is sometimes used.
- In algebra, an _____ or _____ element of a set S with a binary operation Â· is an element e that, when combined with any element x of S, produces that same x. That is, eÂ·x = xÂ·e = x for all x in S.
    - The _____ function from a set S to itself, often denoted id or $id_S$, s the function such that i = x for all x in S. This function serves as the _____ element in the set of all functions from S to itself with respect to function composition.
    - In linear algebra, the _____ matrix of size n is the n-by-n square matrix with ones on the main diagonal and zeros elsewhere. This matrix serves as the _____ with respect to matrix multiplication.

A common example of the first meaning is the trigonometric _____

$$\sin^2 \theta + \cos^2 \theta = 1$$

which is true for all real values of θ, as opposed to

$$\cos \theta = 1,$$

which is true only for some values of θ, not all. For example, the latter equation is true when $\theta = 0$, false when $\theta = 2$

The concepts of 'additive _____' and 'multiplicative _____' are central to the Peano axioms. The number 0 is the 'additive _____' for integers, real numbers, and complex numbers. For the real numbers, for all $a \in \mathbb{R}$,

$$0 + a = a,$$

$$a + 0 = a, \text{ and}$$

$$0 + 0 = 0.$$

Similarly, The number 1 is the 'multiplicative _____' for integers, real numbers, and complex numbers.

a. ARIA
b. Action
c. Identity
d. Intersection

## Chapter 8. The Real Numbers

10. _____ is the mathematical operation of scaling one number by another. It is one of the four basic operations in elementary arithmetic.

_____ is defined for whole numbers in terms of repeated addition; for example, 4 multiplied by 3 can be calculated by adding 3 copies of 4 together:

$$4 + 4 + 4 = 12.$$

_____ of rational numbers and real numbers is defined by systematic generalization of this basic idea.

a. Least common multiple
b. The number 0 is even.
c. Highest common factor
d. Multiplication


11. In mathematics the _____ of a set which is equipped with the operation of addition is an element which, when added to any element x in the set, yields x. One of the most familiar additive identities is the number 0 from elementary mathematics, but additive identities occur in other mathematical structures where addition is defined, such as in groups and rings.

- The _____ familiar from elementary mathematics is zero, denoted 0. For example,

    5 + 0 = 5 = 0 + 5.

- In the natural numbers N and all of its supersets, the _____ is 0. Thus for any one of these numbers n,

    n + 0 = n = 0 + n.

Let N be a set which is closed under the operation of addition, denoted +. An _____ for N is any element e such that for any element n in N,

   e + n = n = n + e.

a. Unit ring
b. Additive Identity
c. Algebraically independent
d. Unique factorization domain

## Chapter 8. The Real Numbers

12. In mathematics, a _____ of a number x is a number r such that $r^2$ = x, or, in other words, a number r whose square is x. Every non-negative real number x has a unique non-negative _____, called the principal _____, which is denoted with a radical symbol as $\sqrt{x}$, or, using exponent notation, as $x^{1/2}$. For example, the principal _____ of 9 is 3, denoted $\sqrt{9}$ = 3, because $3^2$ = 3 × 3 = 9.
    a. Double exponential
    b. Square root
    c. Multiplicative inverse
    d. Hyperbolic functions

13. In mathematics and logic, the phrase 'there is one and only one' is used to indicate that exactly one object with a certain property exists. In mathematical logic, this sort of quantification is known as _____ quantification or unique existential quantification.

    _____ quantification is often denoted with the symbols '∃!' or '∃$_{=1}$'.

    a. A posteriori
    b. A chemical equation
    c. A Mathematical Theory of Communication
    d. Uniqueness

14. In vascular plants, the _____ is the organ of a plant body that typically lies below the surface of the soil. This is not always the case, however, since a _____ can also be aerial (that is, growing above the ground) or aerating (that is, growing up above the ground or especially above water.) Furthermore, a stem normally occurring below ground is not exceptional either
    a. Root
    b. 120-cell
    c. 1-center problem
    d. 2-3 heap

15. In mathematics, a _____ is a statement that can be proved on the basis of explicitly stated or previously agreed assumptions.
    a. Boolean function
    b. Disjunction introduction
    c. Theorem
    d. Logical value

## Chapter 8. The Real Numbers

16. In mathematics, an _____ in the sense of ring theory is a subring $\mathcal{O}$ of a ring R that satisfies the conditions

   1. R is a ring which is a finite-dimensional algebra over the rational number field $\mathbb{Q}$
   2. $\mathcal{O}$ spans R over $\mathbb{Q}$, so that $\mathbb{Q}\mathcal{O} = R$, and
   3. $\mathcal{O}$ is a lattice in R.

The third condition can be stated more accurately, in terms of the extension of scalars of R to the real numbers, embedding R in a real vector space. In less formal terms, additively $\mathcal{O}$ should be a free abelian group generated by a basis for R over $\mathbb{Q}$.

The leading example is the case where R is a number field K and $\mathcal{O}$ is its ring of integers. In algebraic number theory there are examples for any K other than the rational field of proper subrings of the ring of integers that are also _____s.

   a. Efficiency
   b. Algebraic
   c. Annihilator
   d. Order


17. In mathematics and set theory, a total order, linear order, simple order, or
   a. Triadic relation
   b. Totally ordered set
   c. Linear order
   d. Cyclic order


18. In quantum field theory and statistical mechanics in the thermodynamic limit, a system with a global symmetry can have more than one phase. For parameters where the symmetry is spontaneously broken, the system is said to be _____. When the global symmetry is unbroken the system is disordered.
   a. Ursell function
   b. Einstein relation
   c. Isoenthalpic-isobaric ensemble
   d. Ordered


19. In mathematics, the _____ of a real number is its numerical value without regard to its sign. So, for example, 3 is the _____ of both 3 and −3.

The _____ of a number a is denoted by $|a|$.

Generalizations of the _____ for real numbers occur in a wide variety of mathematical settings.

## Chapter 8. The Real Numbers

a. Area hyperbolic functions
b. Absolute value
c. A chemical equation
d. A Mathematical Theory of Communication

20. The _____ are the set of numbers consisting of the natural numbers including 0 and their negatives. They are numbers that can be written without a fractional or decimal component, and fall within the set {... −2, −1, 0, 1, 2, ...}.

a. Integers
b. A Mathematical Theory of Communication
c. A posteriori
d. A chemical equation

21. In mathematics, a _____ is a number which can be expressed as a ratio of two integers. Non-integer _____s are usually written as the vulgar fraction $\frac{a}{b}$, where b is not zero. a is called the numerator, and b the denominator.

a. Rational number
b. Pre-algebra
c. Minkowski distance
d. Tally marks

22. In mathematics, especially in order theory, the _____ of a subset S of a partially ordered set (poset) is an element of S which is greater than or equal to any other element of S. The term least element is defined dually. A bounded poset is a poset that has both a _____ and a least element.

a. Supremum
b. Majorization
c. Lower bound
d. Greatest element

23. In mathematics the infimum of a subset of some set is the greatest element, not necessarily in the subset, that is less than or equal to all elements of the subset. Consequently the term _____ is also commonly used. Infima of real numbers are a common special case that is especially important in analysis.

a. Supremum
b. Strict weak ordering
c. Strong antichain
d. Greatest lower bound

24. In mathematics, given a subset S of a partially ordered set T, the supremum (sup) of S, if it exists, is the least element of T that is greater than or equal to each element of S. Consequently, the supremum is also referred to as the _____, lub or _____. If the supremum exists, it may or may not belong to S.
   a. Complete Heyting algebra
   b. Compact element
   c. Supermodular
   d. Least upper bound


25. In mathematics, an _____ or member of a set is any one of the distinct objects that make up that set.

Writing A = {1,2,3,4}, means that the _____s of the set A are the numbers 1, 2, 3 and 4. Groups of _____s of A, for example {1,2}, are subsets of A.

   a. Ideal
   b. Universal code
   c. Order
   d. Element


26. The _____, also abbreviated as the LUB axiom, is an axiom of real analysis stating that if a nonempty subset of the real numbers has an upper bound, then it has a least upper bound. It is an axiom in the sense that it cannot be proven within the system of real analysis. However, like other axioms of classical fields of mathematics, it can be proven from Zermelo-Fraenkel set theory, an external system.
   a. Continuity property
   b. Fundamental axiom of analysis
   c. Least upper bound axiom
   d. Real projective line


27. In mathematics, especially in order theory, an upper bound of a subset S of some partially ordered set is an element of P which is greater than or equal to every element of S. The term _____ is defined dually as an element of P which is lesser than or equal to every element of S. A set with an upper bound is said to be bounded from above by that bound, a set with a _____ is said to be bounded from below by that bound.
   a. Partially ordered set
   b. Lower bound
   c. Cofinality
   d. Monomial order

## Chapter 8. The Real Numbers

28. In mathematics, especially in order theory, an _____ of a subset S of some partially ordered set is an element of P which is greater than or equal to every element of S. The term lower bound is defined dually as an element of P which is lesser than or equal to every element of S. A set with an _____ is said to be bounded from above by that bound, a set with a lower bound is said to be bounded from below by that bound.
   a. Order isomorphism
   b. Order-embedding
   c. Infinite descending chain
   d. Upper bound

29. In mathematics, an _____ is a theorem with a statement beginning 'there exis ..' y, ... there exis ...'. That is, in more formal terms of symbolic logic, it is a theorem with a statement involving the existential quantifier.
   a. A Mathematical Theory of Communication
   b. A chemical equation
   c. A posteriori
   d. Existence theorem

30. In mathematics, the _____ of a set is a measure of the 'number of elements of the set'. For example, the set A = {1, 2, 3} contains 3 elements, and therefore A has a _____ of 3. There are two approaches to _____ - one which compares sets directly using bijections and injections, and another which uses cardinal numbers.
   a. 120-cell
   b. 2-3 heap
   c. 1-center problem
   d. Cardinality

31. In mathematics, a _____ is a set where a notion of distance (called a metric) between elements of the set is defined.

The _____ which most closely corresponds to our intuitive understanding of space is the 3-dimensional Euclidean space. In fact, the notion of 'metric' is a generalization of the Euclidean metric arising from the four long known properties of the Euclidean distance.

   a. 2-3 heap
   b. 120-cell
   c. 1-center problem
   d. Metric space

32. The mathematical concept of a _____ expresses the intuitive idea of deterministic dependence between two quantities, one of which is viewed as primary and the other as secondary. A _____ then is a way to associate a unique output for each input of a specified type, for example, a real number or an element of a given set.

   a. Going up
   b. Coherent
   c. Grill
   d. Function

33. In mathematics, a _____, named after Augustin Cauchy, is a sequence whose elements become arbitrarily close to each other as the sequence progresses. To be more precise, by dropping enough terms from the start of the sequence, it is possible to make the maximum of the distances from any of the remaining elements to any other such element smaller than any preassigned positive value.

In other words, suppose a pre-assigned positive real value $\varepsilon$ is chosen.

   a. Hausdorff distance
   b. Contraction mapping
   c. Cauchy sequence
   d. Systolic inequalities for curves on surfaces

34. In general, an object is complete if nothing needs to be added to it. This notion is made more specific in various fields.

In logic, semantic _____ is the converse of soundness for formal systems.

   a. Giuseppe Peano
   b. Set theory
   c. Completeness
   d. Logical equality

35. _____ is the branch of mathematics that studies sets, which are collections of objects. Although any type of objects can be collected into a set, _____ is applied most often to objects that are relevant to mathematics.

The modern study of _____ was initiated by Cantor and Dedekind in the 1870s.

   a. Consistent
   b. Logical conjunction
   c. Set theory
   d. Logical value

## Chapter 8. The Real Numbers

36. The word _____ has many distinct meanings in different fields of knowledge, depending on their methodologies and the context of discussion. Broadly speaking we can say that a _____ is some kind of belief or claim that (supposedly) explains, asserts, or consolidates some class of claims. Additionally, in contrast with a theorem the statement of the _____ is generally accepted only in some tentative fashion as opposed to regarding it as having been conclusively established.
   a. Per mil
   b. Transport of structure
   c. Theory
   d. Defined

37. In mathematical logic, an _____ generalizes the notion of axiom.

An _____ is a formula in the language of an axiomatic system, in which one or more schematic variables appear. These variables, which are metalinguistic constructs, stand for any term or subformula of the system, which may or may not be required to satisfy certain conditions.

   a. Axiom schema
   b. A Mathematical Theory of Communication
   c. A posteriori
   d. A chemical equation

38. In mathematics, and more specifically set theory, the _____ is the unique set having no members. Some axiomatic set theories assure that the _____ exists by including an axiom of _____; in other theories, its existence can be deduced. Many possible properties of sets are trivially true for the _____.
   a. Inverse function
   b. Empty function
   c. A Mathematical Theory of Communication
   d. Empty set

39. In logic, _____ refers to principles that judge objects to be equal if they have the same external properties. It is the opposite concept of intensionality, which is concerned with whether two descriptions are intended to be the same or not.

Consider the functions f and g from the natural numbers to the natural numbers defined as follows:

- To find f(n), first add 5 to n, then multiply by 2.
- To find g(n), first multiply n by 2, then add 10.

These functions are extensionally equal; given the same input, both functions always produce the same value. But the definitions of the functions are not equal, and in that intensional sense the functions are not the same.

a. Ordinal arithmetic
b. Infinitary combinatorics
c. A Mathematical Theory of Communication
d. Extensionality

40. In regression analysis and related fields such as econometrics, _____ is the process of converting a theory into a regression model. This process consists of selecting an appropriate functional form for the model and choosing which variables to include. Model _____ is one of the first steps in regression analysis.
a. Mean response
b. Feasible generalized least squares
c. Smoothing spline
d. Specification

41. In mathematics, the _____ of two sets A and B is the set that contains all elements of A that also belong to B, but no other elements.

For explanation of the symbols used in this article, refer to the table of mathematical symbols.

The _____ of A and B

The _____ of A and B is written 'A ∩ B'. Formally:

   x is an element of A ∩ B if and only if
   - x is an element of A and
   - x is an element of B.
   For example:
   - The _____ of the sets {1, 2, 3} and {2, 3, 4} is {2, 3}.
   - The number 9 is not in the _____ of the set of prime numbers {2, 3, 5, 7, 11, …} and the set of odd numbers {1, 3, 5, 7, 9, 11, …}.

If the _____ of two sets A and B is empty, that is they have no elements in common, then they are said to be disjoint, denoted: A ∩ B = ∅. For example the sets {1, 2} and {3, 4} are disjoint, written {1, 2} ∩ {3, 4} = ∅.

a. Intersection
b. Order
c. Advice
d. Erlang

## Chapter 8. The Real Numbers

42. The concept of _____ treated here occurs in mathematics.

Let R be a commutative ring with unity, and let M, N and L be three R-modules.

A _____ is any R-bilinear map $e : M \times N \to L$.

   a. Standard basis
   b. Direct sum
   c. Coordinate space
   d. Pairing


43. In set theory, the term _____ refers to a set operation used in the convergence of set elements to form a resultant set containing the elements of both sets. As a simple example, a _____ of two disjoint sets, which do not have elements in common results in a set containing all elements from both sets. A Venn diagram representing the _____ of sets A and B.

   a. Union
   b. Introduction
   c. Event
   d. UES


44. In mathematics, an _____ is a collection of objects having two coordinates (or entries or projections), such that one can always uniquely determine the object, which is the first coordinate (or first entry or left projection) of the pair as well as the second coordinate (or second entry or right projection.) If the first coordinate is a and the second is b, the usual notation for an _____ is (a, b.) The pair is 'ordered' in that (a, b) differs from (b, a) unless a = b.

   a. A Mathematical Theory of Communication
   b. A posteriori
   c. A chemical equation
   d. Ordered pair


45. In mathematics, given a set S, the _____ of S, written $\mathcal{P}(S)$, PS, is the set of all subsets of S. In axiomatic set theory, the existence of the _____ of any set is postulated by the axiom of _____.

Any subset F of $\mathcal{P}(S)$ is called a family of sets over S.

## Chapter 8. The Real Numbers

a. Formal power series
b. Formal derivative
c. Polarization
d. Power set

46. In mathematics, the _____ is a direct product of sets. The _____ is named after René Descartes, whose formulation of analytic geometry gave rise to this concept.

Specifically, the _____ of two sets X and Y, denoted X × Y, is the set of all possible ordered pairs whose first component is a member of X and whose second component is a member of Y:

$$X \times Y = \{(x,y) | x \in X \text{ and } y \in Y\}.$$

For example, the _____ of the 13-element set of standard playing card ranks {Ace, King, Queen, Jack, 10, 9, 8, 7, 6, 5, 4, 3, 2} and the four-element set of card suits {â™ , â™¥, â™¦, â™£} is the 52-element set of all possible playing cards ,, ....,,, ....,}.

a. Cartesian product
b. Choice function
c. Set of all sets
d. Disjoint sets

47. In descriptive set theory, an _____ of real numbers is one that can be defined as the least fixed point of a monotone operation definable by a positive $\Sigma^1_n$ formula, for some natural number n, together with a real parameter.

The _____s form a boldface pointclass; that is, they are closed under continuous preimages. In the Wadge hierarchy, they lie above the projective sets and below the sets in .

a. Inductive set
b. A Mathematical Theory of Communication
c. Attributional calculus
d. Elementary embedding

48. _____ is the state of being greater than any finite number, however large.

## Chapter 8. The Real Numbers

a. Implicit differentiation
b. A Mathematical Theory of Communication
c. Infinity
d. Interval notation


49. In mathematics, a _____ can mean either an element of the set {1, 2, 3, ...} or an element of the set {0, 1, 2, 3, ...}. The latter is especially preferred in mathematical logic, set theory, and computer science.

_____s have two main purposes: they can be used for counting, and they can be used for ordering.

a. Cardinal numbers
b. Suslin cardinal
c. Strong partition cardinal
d. Natural number


50. In set theory, a set (or class) A is transitive, if

- whenever x ∈ A, and y ∈ x, then y ∈ A, or, equivalently,
- whenever x ∈ A, and x is not an urelement, then x is a subset of A.

The transitive closure of a set A is the smallest (with respect to inclusion) _____ B which contains A. Suppose one is given a set X, then the transitive closure of X is:

$$\bigcup \{X, \bigcup X, \bigcup\bigcup X, \bigcup\bigcup\bigcup X, \bigcup\bigcup\bigcup\bigcup X, ...\}$$

Transitive classes are often used for construction of interpretations of set theory in itself, usually called inner models. The reason is that properties defined by bounded formulas are absolute for transitive classes.

a. Quasi-set theory
b. Transitive set
c. Club set
d. Hartogs number


51. In mathematical logic, the _____ are a set of axioms for the natural numbers presented by the 19th century Italian mathematician Giuseppe Peano. These axioms have been used nearly unchanged in a number of metamathematical investigations, including research into fundamental questions of consistency and completeness of number theory.

# Chapter 8. The Real Numbers

The need for formalism in arithmetic was not well appreciated until the work of Hermann Grassmann, who showed in the 1860s that many facts in arithmetic could be derived from more basic facts about the successor operation and induction.

a. Presburger arithmetic
b. Special relativity
c. Systolic geometry
d. Peano axioms

52. _____, in mathematics and computer science, is a method of defining functions in which the function being defined is applied within its own definition. The term is also used more generally to describe a process of repeating objects in a self-similar way. For instance, when the surfaces of two mirrors are almost parallel with each other the nested images that occur are a form of _____.

a. 2-3 heap
b. Recursion
c. 1-center problem
d. 120-cell

53. _____ consists of the mental process of thinking involved with the process of judging the merits of multiple options and selecting one of them for action. Some simple examples include deciding whether to get up in the morning or go back to sleep, or selecting a given route for a journey. More complex examples include choosing a lifestyle, religious affiliation, or political position.

a. Decision analysis
b. Decision Matrix
c. Choice
d. James-Stein estimator

54.

A _____ (selector, selection) is a mathematical function f whose domain X is a collection of nonempty sets such that for every S in X, f(S) is an element of S. In other words f chooses exactly one element from each set in X.

Ernst Zermelo introduced _____s along with the axiom of choice (AC) in a 1904 paper that gave a proof of the well-ordering theorem, which states that every set can be well-ordered.

## Chapter 8. The Real Numbers

a. Preimage
b. Choice function
c. Disjoint union
d. Horizontal line test


55. An _____ is an artifact, usually two-dimensional (a picture), that has a similar appearance to some subject--usually a physical object or a person.

_____s may be two-dimensional, such as a photograph, screen display, and as well as a three-dimensional, such as a statue. They may be captured by optical devices--such as cameras, mirrors, lenses, telescopes, microscopes, etc.

a. A posteriori
b. A Mathematical Theory of Communication
c. A chemical equation
d. Image


56. In mathematics, an _____ is a binary relation between two elements of a set which groups them together as being 'equivalent' in some way. Let a, b, and c be arbitrary elements of some set X. Then 'a ~ b' or 'a ≡ b' denotes that a is equivalent to b.

a. Equivalence class
b. A chemical equation
c. Equivalence relation
d. A Mathematical Theory of Communication


57. In mathematics, a _____, named after Richard Dedekind, in a totally ordered set S is a partition of it into two non-empty parts,, such that A is closed downwards and B is closed upwards, and A contains no greatest element. The cut itself is, conceptually, the 'gap' defined between A and B. See also completeness.

a. Majorization
b. Preordered class
c. Non-increasing sequence
d. Dedekind cut

## Chapter 1
1. c   2. b   3. d   4. d   5. a   6. d   7. b   8. b   9. b   10. b
11. b  12. d  13. b  14. d  15. d  16. a  17. b  18. c  19. c

## Chapter 2
1. b   2. d   3. d   4. d   5. d   6. d   7. d   8. d   9. d   10. b
11. d  12. d  13. d  14. d  15. d  16. d  17. b  18. d  19. d  20. d
21. a  22. d

## Chapter 3
1. a   2. d   3. a   4. b

## Chapter 4
1. a   2. d   3. a   4. d   5. d   6. c   7. d   8. d   9. a   10. b
11. c  12. b  13. c  14. c  15. a  16. d  17. d  18. a  19. d  20. d
21. b  22. a  23. d  24. a  25. b  26. b  27. d  28. c  29. d  30. b
31. d  32. d  33. d  34. a  35. a  36. a  37. b  38. b  39. a  40. d
41. c  42. d  43. c  44. d

## Chapter 5
1. d   2. a   3. d   4. c   5. d   6. d   7. a   8. d   9. d   10. d
11. c  12. a  13. d  14. c  15. d  16. b  17. d  18. d  19. b  20. a
21. d  22. b  23. a  24. a  25. c  26. d  27. b  28. d  29. b

## Chapter 6
1. a   2. d   3. b   4. c   5. d   6. b   7. d   8. a   9. b   10. d
11. d  12. d  13. d  14. a  15. d  16. d  17. d  18. a  19. d  20. d
21. d  22. a  23. d  24. d  25. d  26. a  27. d  28. d  29. d  30. d
31. c  32. d  33. d  34. d  35. d

## Chapter 7
1. c   2. d   3. a   4. b   5. d   6. b   7. b   8. a   9. d   10. a
11. d  12. c  13. c  14. d  15. d  16. d  17. d  18. a  19. d  20. d
21. d  22. c  23. a  24. c  25. d  26. b  27. a  28. a  29. d  30. b

## Chapter 8
1. b   2. d   3. d   4. d   5. d   6. a   7. d   8. d   9. c   10. d
11. b  12. b  13. d  14. a  15. c  16. d  17. b  18. d  19. b  20. a
21. a  22. d  23. d  24. d  25. d  26. c  27. b  28. d  29. d  30. d
31. d  32. d  33. c  34. c  35. c  36. c  37. a  38. d  39. d  40. d
41. a  42. d  43. a  44. d  45. d  46. a  47. a  48. c  49. d  50. b
51. d  52. b  53. c  54. b  55. d  56. c  57. d